Public Relations Ethics

Public Relations Ethics

Senior PR Pros Tell Us How to Speak Up and Keep Your Job

Marlene S. Neill and Amy Oliver Barnes

Public Relations Ethics: Senior PR Pros Tell Us How to Speak Up and Keep Your Job

First published in 2018 by
Business Expert Press, LLC
222 East 46th Street, New York, NY 10017
www.businessexpertpress.com

ISBN-13: 978-1-94709-864-0 (paperback)
ISBN-13: 978-1-94709-865-7 (e-book)

Business Expert Press Public Relations Collection

Collection ISSN: 2157-345X (print)
Collection ISSN: 2157-3476 (electronic)

Cover and interior design by Exeter Premedia Services Private Ltd., Chennai, India

First edition: 2018

10 9 8 7 6 5 4 3 2 1

Printed in the United States of America.

Abstract

Many senior public relations executives consider ethics counsel to be one of their core responsibilities since ethical conduct is associated with trust and credibility. Raising ethical concerns to more senior leaders, however, can be quite intimidating. The reality is that, often, "speaking truth to power" can have serious consequences for someone's career. For these reasons, senior public relations executives have mastered the art of using less confrontational strategies to approach their superiors. This book ranks and describes these various strategies and offers specific examples of how public relations executives have used them in practice. The insights are based on nearly 150 in-depth interviews with public relations executives—professionals working in a variety of industries, as well as original survey research. Readers learn about the process of gaining influence and the mistakes to avoid when navigating internal politics. For young professionals interested in advancing into management, this book is a must read, not only for the advice from senior professionals about issues that can be career altering, but also because that advice covers topics that few actually talk about. While this book specifically examines influence and counsel from an ethics perspective, many of the lessons are applicable to public relations counsel generally.

Keywords

allies, coalitions, corporate communication, ethical culture, ethical leadership, ethics, influence, internal politics, mentors, public relations, social capital, whistleblowers

Contents

Preface

Since advice based on experience is often the most valuable advice, for this book we sought insights from senior public relations executives about successfully raising ethical concerns to senior leaders. While our focus is ethics counsel, some of the lessons learned can be applied to public relations counsel generally. Additionally, these senior public relations leaders provide guidance for gaining influence in a company or organization, which is essential for any effective public relations strategy. These insights are based on nearly 150 interviews and survey research conducted over several years. This project began as a follow-up to 2012 published research conducted by Neill and Drumwright, which involved in-depth interviews with 30 public relations executives. Occasionally, we include some quotes from that study as well, some of which have never been previously published.

We also include findings from a second study, which was conducted in 2012 by Neill and involved 30 in-depth interviews with senior executives working in four different U.S. companies. That study provides additional insights for navigating internal politics (see Chapter 5). A third study, published in 2016 by Neill, was based on in-depth interviews with 32 professionals specializing in internal communication to discover recommendations for building an ethical culture (see Chapter 8).

Finally, in preparation for this book, we gathered new data—including 34 in-depth interviews with members of the PRSA College of Fellows and 21 current and former members of the Arthur W. Page Society, representing more than 40 hours of new insights. The PRSA College of Fellows is an exclusive group of approximately 350 senior professionals, each with a minimum of 20 years of experience in public relations, accreditation (APR), and recognition for distinguished careers in public relations. The PRSA Fellows interviewed had an average of 35 years of experience in public relations. The Page Society is an elite group as well, open by invitation only to chief communications officers (CCOs) of Fortune 500 corporations and leading nonprofit organizations, the CEOs of public relations agencies, and senior professors from business and communications schools. The current and former Page Society members interviewed had an average 30 years of experience in public relations. Due to the sensitive and confidential nature of the issues discussed, we agreed not to name the participants, so they will only be identified as a PRSA Fellow or Page Society member and by gender, when appropriate. We also conducted survey research with PRSA Fellows and members of the Southern Public Relations Federation (SPRF), with a sample of 72 participants (33 PRSA Fellows and 39 SPRF).

Acknowledgments

We would like to thank the many individuals who helped us complete this book, beginning with the senior public relations executives who set aside time to be interviewed for this study. We also appreciate the support of the reviewers and editors at Business Expert Press throughout the process including Drs Don W. Stacks and Donald K. Wright. We are grateful to the Arthur W. Page Center for Integrity in Public Communication, which provided grant funding for this project. We also would like to express appreciation to the PRSA Board of Ethics and Professional Standards, the PRSA College of Fellows, and Southern Public Relations Federation for their support of this study. All of these efforts were made possible due to the support of our employers, Baylor University and the University of Arkansas-Little Rock. Finally, thank you to Drs Bruce Berger and Bryan Reber, whose prior research provided the inspiration for this project.

—**Marlene S. Neill and Amy Oliver Barnes**

Outline of Book

The first two chapters introduce readers to the concept of an ethical conscience in public relations and associated responsibilities, as well as what influence in public relations means.

Chapter 3 focuses on the importance of building relationships with colleagues within a company or organization, and why it must be a prerequisite for serving as an ethics counselor. Readers will learn about specific ways they can approach more senior colleagues in order to build trusting relationships.

Chapters 4 to 6 provide insight into the different strategies public relations executives use to provide ethics counsel, some of which are non-confrontational and others which are high stakes and could have lasting effects on someone's career. The senior executives discuss specific examples of times when they used these various strategies.

Chapter 7 provides advice for young professionals who are preparing for the challenges of ethics counsel, especially counseling senior leaders. The chapter also features discussions on the importance of training and the need to identify and seek counsel from mentors.

Chapter 8 presents six recommendations for building an ethical culture, along with guidance about how public relations professionals can lead and contribute to those efforts.

Chapter 9 shares words of wisdom for students and young professionals from the senior executives interviewed. The senior executives addressed topics such as ways to improve business literacy, the importance of researching potential clients and employers, what it means to provide ethical leadership, and mistakes to avoid.

Finally, Chapter 10 offers ten practices young professionals and future professionals should make part of their daily and monthly routines to remain ethically sharp and influential.

Each chapter ends with a summary and questions to consider.

Additionally, four appendices are provided that give a summary of quantitative results from the surveys and interviews presented throughout this book.

CHAPTER 1

Why Does Ethics Matter in Public Relations?

Both public relations employers and educators rank ethics among the most essential competencies for aspiring professionals to master (DiStaso, Stacks, and Botan 2009; Todd 2009). Many senior public relations executives even describe ethics as the foundation of effective public relations. For Anthony D'Angelo, 2017 Chair-Elect for the Public Relations Society of America (PRSA), ethics are essential to the practice:

> As the late Patrick Jackson wisely noted, the currency of public relations is relationships. I think, essential to that currency, in order to make it work, the bedrock has to be trust…built on an ethical foundation and once trust is broken, you can't have effective public relations, nor can you have an effective organization. So it's really a central, important, grave responsibility.

Part of the foundation of ethics in public relations is truthful communication. As a PRSA Fellow working in an agency setting noted:

> It means that the communications we give…will be believable, it will be truthful, it will not be deceitful, it will be in the public interest, but it also will be in the clients' interest too. But we will not sacrifice the standards of truth and good communications just to satisfy a client.

Most college students will learn about ethics while studying philosophy or professional codes of ethics. One or two ethics courses, however, does not begin to prepare public relations professionals for the responsibility many in the profession have called an "ethical conscience." While many of us might recall a conscience illustrated by the fictional childhood character Jiminy Cricket as he tried to prevent Pinocchio from making mistakes, this example, would have been far too simple for moral development philosophers.

Developing a Conscience

Moral development begins in early childhood, primarily from interaction with our parents. As we mature, we advance to higher levels of moral development. Although Piaget (1997) identified four stages (e.g., ritualized schema, egocentric, cooperation, and codification of rules), Kohlberg (1969) focused on six potential stages of moral development (see Table 1.1). Kohlberg's stages offer additional insight into moral development and are discussed below.

Table 1.1 Kohlberg's stages of moral development

Basis of moral judgment	Stages of development	Motivation for moral behavior
Level 1: Moral value is external, in bad acts, rather than in persons	**Stage 1:** Obedience and punishment orientation	**Stage 1:** Avoiding punishment
	Stage 2: Naively egoistic orientation—right action is one which satisfies the self's needs and occasionally others' needs	**Stage 2:** A desire for reward or benefit
Level 2: Moral value involves performing good or right roles, maintaining order and meeting the expectations of others	**Stage 3:** Good-boy orientation—focus is on approval and pleasing and helping others	**Stage 3:** Potential disapproval of others
	Stage 4: Authority and maintaining social-order orientation—focused on duty, showing respect to those in authority	**Stage 4:** Potential disgrace or failure
Level 3: Moral value resides in conformity with shared standards such as codes of ethics, rights, or duties	**Stage 5:** Contractual legalistic orientation—duty defined in terms of contract, focused on protecting the rights of others	**Stage 5:** Concerned with public interest and own self-respect

	Stage 6: Conscience or principle orientation— appeal to universality, consistency, mutual respect and trust	**Stage 6:** Concerned about violating one's own principles

Several terms have been used to describe the first stage, including compliance, obedience, and punishment orientations (Kelman 1961; Piaget 1997; Rest, Turiel, and Kohlberg 1969). This stage focuses on our willingness to obey others' rules to avoid punishment or receive rewards. Obviously, this implies behavior is dependent on the presence of others (Kochanska and Aksan 2006), and because the rules are not part of the individual's personal conscience, they do not fully influence behavior (Piaget 1997). This stage also has been referred to as primary socialization (Berger and Luckmann 1967).

The next stage is identification, when an individual adopts behavior to build and maintain relationships with another person or group (Kelman 1961); a process called secondary socialization (Berger and Luckmann 1967). Kohlberg (1969) wrote that identification applies across a variety of situations and behaviors. He also found it to be persistent, occurring when others are not around, and even without reinforcement. This stage represents Kohlberg's (1969) egoistic orientation (stage 2) and good-boy orientation (stage 3). Egoistic orientation focuses on compliance in order to receive rewards or benefits, while the good-boy orientation seeks approval through pleasing and helping others (Kohlberg 1969). Similarly, Piaget (1997) referred to these stages as egocentric and cooperation. From a child's perspective, rules are regarded as sacred and untouchable and as a form of loyalty.

Kohlberg's (1969) fourth stage, the authority and maintaining social-order orientation stage, focuses on duty and respect for authority. Similarly, Piaget (1997) calls this stage codification of rules. It is at this stage that concepts such as social norms and descriptive norms become important for predicting behavior. Social norms are "rules and standards that are understood by members of a group and that guide and/or constrain social behavior without the force of laws" (Cialdini and Trost 1998, p. 152). Industry codes of ethics would be a good example of social norms.

Descriptive norms (i.e., what is actually done) motivate us to imitate the behavior of those who have visible signs of success such as wealth, power, or status (Cialdini and Trost 1998).

Eventually some rules are internalized as personal norms (Cialdini and Trost 1998), becoming part of our values system (Kelman 1961). This would be consistent with Kohlberg's (1969) fifth and sixth stages of development, when a person considers issues such as duty, rights of others, and universal principles. This is the level of moral development that we refer to as a *conscience*, that which is "embedded in the self, so as to become an internal guideline for the necessary personal decisions of social life…what gives us the courage of our convictions" (Miltch and Orange 2004, p. 207). These convictions can be referred to as the values or guiding principles in our lives (Schwartz 1996). Values represent "enduring notions of goodness and badness that guide behavior in a variety of contexts," and are usually resistant to change (Burgoon 1989, p. 132). While some people may think the conscience plays a role in most decision making, Rest et al. (1969) suggest that the majority of U.S. adults make moral judgments at the Kohlberg's conventional (stages 3 and 4) levels, based on the good-boy orientation and maintaining social order.

In contrast to the more self-centered motivations for ethical behavior, we found some professionals who are accredited in public relations (i.e., hold the "APR" designation) and have internalized the PRSA *Code of Ethics* (https://prsa.org/ethics/code-of-ethics/) to the point that the principles and values of the code are consistent with their own values. As a PRSA Fellow, who was a principal in an agency explained, the code was part of the agency's normal business practices:

> There was only three partners—one left I became the third partner. And from day one, because I was APR, I insisted on putting in our proposals and in our letters of agreement with the clients, that we published the PRSA *Code of Ethics* and each of the partners would sign to have this—this is how we're running business with you and for you. So that minimized the number of (ethics) discussions we ever had to have.

Further evidence of internalization and identification with the PRSA *Code of Ethics* was obvious in an interview with a female senior executive, an APR, who recalled the time her boss asked her to share false information in a news release to counter damaging information about the company:

> I gave her four different choices…let's reword the press release, let's leave out the information that she perceived was damaging, although, I didn't perceive it that way, but anyway, a number of choices…She wanted to issue it that way…So in that instance… my final option to her was let's take my name off of this one and put your name on it and that was met with a red face and I think what she said was, "Are you refusing to do the job for which we hired you?" And I said, "I wouldn't say that I'm refusing to do the job for which you hired me because…you hired me knowing I was an APR, that's the job." (Neill and Drumwright 2012)

Cruising on Autopilot

History has unfortunately given us too many examples of instances when ethics played a minor, if any, role in an executive's decisions or actions. Scholars suggest Schema theory might have been at work in those instances. Schema are those subconscious routines that allow us to function every day, and Schema theory proposes that sometimes scripts or action rules, or "cruising on automatic pilot," guide our behavior (Ableson 1982). By using scripts, "a decision maker need not actively think about each new presentation of information, situations, or problems; the mode of handling such problems has already been worked out in advance" (Gioia 1992, p. 386). In fact, Schwartz (1996) wrote that "values may play little role in behavior except when there is a value conflict," otherwise "habitual, scripted responses may suffice" (p. 2).

Those habitual, autopilot responses were a fear for one senior public relations executive working in an agency setting:

> I think the greatest concern I have is just…in the midst of all the things that you do in your professional life, are your ethical antennas up sufficiently high to see a potential concern and then place it on the table for review, debate, discussion. (Neill and Drumwright 2012)

The Process of Ethical Decision Making

Just as it is helpful to understand how a conscience is formed, it is also beneficial to examine the steps involved in making an ethical decision. Ethics have been described as "a systematic attempt to make sense of our individual and social moral experience, to determine the rules that ought to govern human conduct, the values worth pursuing, and the character traits deserving development in life" (DeGeorge 2009, p. 13). In practice, ethical decision making "involves making rational choices between what is good and bad, between what is morally justifiable action and what is not" (Patterson and Wilkins 2005, p. 4). Public relations professionals can draw upon ethical principles based on fundamental values to help them "judge the rightness of decisions" and to resolve conflicting duties to the public and key stakeholders (Fitzpatrick and Gauthier 2001, p. 201). They may consider principles and values drawn from their family and religious upbringing, as well as industry and employer's codes of ethics (Fitzpatrick 2002; Halff 2010; Lee and Cheng 2011; Wright 1993) to lead them to a decision. Examples of core values that are foundational to the PRSA *Code of Ethics* are honesty, loyalty, and fairness. One PRSA Fellow said, "Joe Truncale [CEO of PRSA] had mentioned them at the Leadership Assembly in 2015, and I wrote them down, because they were like just wonderful guidelines to live by." Another PRSA Fellow described the progression of training he has received that guides his ethical decision making:

> I went to a Jesuit university, I was raised a Catholic...I think my mom made sure that I had the understanding of what a moral and ethical lifestyle was all about. And then essentially with teachings of the Catholic church that combined with you know the Jesuit tradition: five philosophy courses, three theology courses and what I would consider a super liberal arts education...set me up for it and then after I got into the profession and joined PRSA back in '78 or whatever...and going for APR...put me in a sequence that had at least some memorization of the [PRSA] *Code of Ethics*... So I think that was an overall sort of lifestyle understanding and training from home to university...basically innate stuff that's in your head that says what's right and what's wrong.

To understand the process we might go through when putting those ethical principles from industry codes of ethics or our upbringing into practice, Rest (1986) developed a four-step model. During the first stage, *moral recognition*, a person identifies a moral or ethical issue based on his or her awareness of industry codes of ethics or ethics training. Jones (1991) pointed out, however, that "a person who fails to recognize a moral issue will fail to employ moral decision-making schemata" and will instead make the decision based on other factors (p. 380). This is what Denny Gioia (1992), Ford Motors' recall coordinator during the Pinto fire crisis of the early 1970s, described when explaining why he chose not to issue a recall after buyers reported a million-and-a-half Pintos with faulty gas tanks. Gioia explained that he was forced to let challenges such as time pressures, production limits, and the market (e.g., oil crisis, lay-offs), rather than ethical considerations, guide his decision.

Once someone recognizes an issue as an ethical one, he or she would then use moral reasoning to make a decision. It is at this stage that some people are able to use *moral imagination*, which Jacobs (1991) described as "articulating and examining alternatives, weighing them and their probable implications, considering their effects on one's other plans and interests, and considering their effects on the interests and feelings of others" (p. 25). Some public relations professionals' have demonstrated moral imagination by using creative approaches to raise ethical concerns. One male senior executive staged a mock news conference to demonstrate why it was a bad idea to use an uninformed spokesperson. The ethical issues in this scenario were related to transparency rather than dodging tough questions. As the male senior executive described:

> I played a rather aggressive environmental reporter, but no more aggressive than any good reporter would be. And at the end of 15 minutes of the HR guy being grilled, and pretty much eviscerated, made to look foolish, so the company would look foolish, and like they were hiding stuff and being deliberately obfuscating the issue, the lawyer looked at me and said, "Ok, you convinced me. That's the wrong decision; we need to have someone there who knows what they're talking about." (Neill and Drumwright 2012)

The next step in ethical decision making is referred to as *moral intent*,(3) which Rest (1986) described as giving "priority to moral values above other personal values such that a decision is made to intend to do what is morally right" (pp. 3–4). This stage is consistent with Rawls' (1971) concept of reflective equilibrium, which is "reached after a person has weighed various proposed conceptions and he has either revised his judgments in accord with one of them or held fast to his initial convictions" (p. 48). Moberg and Seabright (2000) provided three alternatives for decision makers as they progress from moral reasoning to moral intent. The first is "tell-and-sell," which involves convincing others of their moral position and the second is "tell and listen," which requires one to consider others' views and possibly refine the original position. As the second option suggests, Goodstein (2000) advised it may be appropriate to reach a compromise with colleagues, because "as individuals are exposed to an array of varying perspectives and multiple values, one's own certainty about the interpretation or application of a principle may lessen, opening up the possibility of accepting alternative perspectives" (p. 811). In short, at times we may not have all the essential details—or may not have weighed other perspectives—that would lead to a better decision. Based on this perspective, moral compromise is not about compromising our integrity, but considering other reasonable options. As one Arthur W. Page Society member explained:[1]

> Sometimes they [legal] come back with a perspective I hadn't considered that if you say it this way it might be misconstrued as X. Ok, I'll go back to the drawing board and come back again with yet again an alternative. But you can't push back and be assertive and constantly pushing if you're not also listening and reshaping…You can't just aggressively advance your viewpoint without also listening and figuring out how you can find that common ground.

---

[1] "The Arthur W. Page Society is a professional association for senior public relations and corporate communications executives [and leading academics] who seek to enrich and strengthen their profession" (www.awpagesociety.com).

Consistent with this Page member's advice, Moberg and Seabright's (2000) third alternative for decision makers is *mutual problem solving* or *negotiation*. Successful negotiation involves not only listening to others' perspectives, but incorporating those considerations into the final decision (Conger 1998). As an illustration of this principle, a PRSA Fellow with experience in government and legal settings described, "By no means did the communications aspect always have more pull. Frequently other interests overruled what I would have done in a vacuum myself unadvised."

One key element in negotiation is personal credibility, earned through expertise and forming strategic relationships (Conger 1998). This does not mean that those who lack the necessary expertise and strong relationships in their organizations, new employees or those working in lower-level positions, for instance, are left without options. They can hire an outside consultant, reach out to coworkers with credibility within the organization to support a position, or conduct research to find data to back the position (Conger 1998). A PRSA Fellow working in an agency setting described the importance of using research to back-up recommendations:

> I've got a presentation in two weeks to the leadership team at this client. I've got the research people who did this national consumer survey that are based in Virginia, they are going to drive down. And that section of the presentation, they will carry the water on because it has more credibility with the client to have this third party make that presentation—not that they wouldn't trust me to deliver the right information or do so well. But there's value in having that third party person who's not dealing with the day to day make that presentation.

The final step in Rest's (1986) ethical decision-making model is *moral* behavior, which he argued some may never achieve: "the person must have sufficient perseverance, ego strength, and implementation skills to be able to follow through on his/her intention to behave morally, to withstand fatigue and flagging will, and to overcome obstacles" (p. 4). He summed up the difficulty of acting on your values as "weakness of the flesh" (p. 15). A Page Society member described the courage it took to speak out against the unethical behavior of a more senior colleague:

I felt it was a duty to say something about it, even it if involved—even if it was at my own personal risk, and it was. So I was willing to take that risk and to fall on my sword if I had to, because of the investment that I personally had made in the reputation of the company and my desire for the company to continue to be able to enjoy its stellar reputation.

Fortunately, she did not face any retaliation or other consequences for speaking up. She added, "That to me was one of the ultimate tests of whether the organization really adhered to its beliefs and its public and private statements."

In addition to fear, real life financial pressures also can serve as barriers, what some have called "golden handcuffs" (Berger 2005). For senior executives, these barriers are usually substantial salaries, benefits, and power. A PRSA Fellow encountered these "handcuffs" early in her career when she confronted a colleague about the earnings report for a publicly traded company:

I can remember going into the CFO after hours and saying, "You know this doesn't seem right." And I remember him saying to me, "It's not my decision. The chairman has told me what I'm to say. I've got kids in college. I have a big mortgage. It's not really against the law. But everybody does it. And this is what we're gonna do and if you're uncomfortable, then you need to make the choice about what's best for you and your future."

Chapter 6 includes insights from senior executives who have confronted similar resistance to ethics counsel.

How Public Relations Professionals Define an Ethical Conscience

While the concept of an ethical conscience has been advanced by scholars and industry leaders for decades (e.g., Bivins 1992; Bowen 2008, 2009; Fitzpatrick and Gauthier 2001; Fitzpatrick 1996; Paluszek 1989; Ryan and Martinson 1983), there has been no clear consensus about what this role should involve in actual practice. One of the clearest and often cited descriptions depicts an ethical or corporate conscience as "a lack of impulsiveness, care in mapping out alternatives and consequences...and awareness of and concern for the effects of one's decision and policies on others" (Goodpaster and Matthews 1982, p. 134).

To better understand the concept of an ethical conscience, in-depth interviews were conducted with 55 members of the PRSA College of Fellows and Arthur W. Page Society. Members of the College of Fellows are accredited by the Universal Accreditation Board (APRs), have a minimum of 20 years of experience in public relations, and have been recognized for distinguished careers in public relations. The Page Society is also an elite group, open by invitation only to chief communications officers (CCOs) of Fortune 500 corporations and notable nonprofit organizations, the CEOs of public relations agencies, and educators representing thought leadership from business and communications schools.

Some of the more common terms the Fellows used to describe this role included encouraging companies and organizations to practice truthful and authentic communication, "pointing out what is right and what is wrong," being "unafraid to raise these questions," representing the concerns of key stakeholders, and informing "senior management...as to the potential ethical impact of their decisions." The role also has been referred to as "a reality check" or the "last common sense checker or gut checker." Page Society members described the role as raising red flags, "ensuring that the organization you work for or support always does the right thing even when it's the toughest thing," and making sure that decisions are grounded in the company's core values.

The role of ethical conscience also was examined through survey research with members of the College of Fellows and Southern Public Relations Federation (SPRF). In response to a survey question, a SPRF member wrote:

> Acting as an ethical conscience should involve keeping in mind the big picture and how the organization's decisions or actions impact all parties involved. Additionally, to keep a company in good standing with the public and the media, a PR professional

should keep in mind every way every person of society could view a situation.

In response to the same question, a PRSA Fellow wrote, "Having the knowledge and the experience to speak knowledgeably about an issue and present coherent, logical and rational alternatives for consideration." In other related questions, 89 percent of the Fellows and SPRF members agree to strongly agree that public relations professionals should provide ethics counsel, and 63 percent answered that they were likely to actually provide ethics counsel in their jobs.

Two major responsibilities associated with the role of ethical conscience include environmental scanning and boundary spanning. *Environmental scanning* involves monitoring traditional and online media "to identify stakeholders who are affected by potential organizational decisions" (Grunig 2006, p. 159). In a 2012 study on public relations' role as an ethical conscience, a male public relations executive working in an agency described public relations as the "eyes and ears of an organization" (Neill and Drumwright 2012). Another male executive with a nonprofit organization described it as "the duty to bring in the other's voice," which is a reference to stakeholders that may be impacted by a company or organization's decisions such as employees, customers, or the local community. In that same study, a female professional used the "canary in a coal mine analogy" to argue that an ethical conscience can be the early warning sign of potential crises.

Boundary spanning follows environmental scanning, allowing public relations professionals to filter information by choosing to act on some, store others, or summarize and interpret the intelligence for senior management (Aldrich and Herker 1977). A male professional working in education described this role as not only having one "foot inside the organization" but also stepping outside the organization to represent the interests and perspectives of external stakeholders (Neill and Drumwright 2012, p. 227). Neill (2014) found that public relations professionals also act as internal boundary spanners by "gathering intelligence across the company's various business units and then 'connecting the dots' to identify strategic decisions that may be inconsistent or not in the company's best interest" (p. 600).

A PRSA Fellow said he often established the role of ethical conscience with the CEO on the first day of employment:

> I had a conversation with the CEO to whom I reported and I said, I am going to take this role on, and you should want me to take this role [ethics counselor] on because there will be instances where…we're going to do something that…we didn't think clearly about, or we had pressure put on us to do that might not have been the best thing if we had thought about it a little more clearly.

He emphasized that these conversations should be behind closed doors:

> And so I walked into his office and I shut the door and I said, We are going to have one of those conversations that we have when we close the door and when we come out of the conversation, we are going to forget we got into an argument or did whatever we did. We're going to have an opinion.

A primary motivation for public relations professionals to embrace the role of ethical conscience is that they are often the spokespersons for their companies or organizations, putting their own credibility on the line as the voice and face of the brand (Neill and Drumwright 2012). A female executive working in higher education warned there was little chance to go back once the line is crossed:

> I've said many times, that I can't afford to lose my credibility that it's all that I have. As a PR professional, it's all we have. And if I lose my credibility here, it's not like you can go just start over with someone else, somewhere else. Credibility is something you can't afford to lose. And so I think that I just made that very clear to them that I cannot lose my integrity, and my credibility. And I just won't. I won't do anything that's going to jeopardize my own reputation as a professional. And that parlays into the organization's best wishes, what's best for the organization as well, because it wouldn't be good for me as the PR person to be lying and be

seen as a liar for my organization. (Neill and Drumwright 2012, p. 225)

This role takes courage as it often involves providing less-than-welcome advice to people who may outrank you. A male public relations professional working in an agency said it is simply our responsibility to "speak truth to power in the sense that our job is not to be yes-men or yes-women." Chapters 4 and 5 provide specific examples from senior executives who have effectively counseled other senior executives while managing to keep their jobs. At the same time, they recognized that they have no control over whether the senior executive accepts their advice, but as a PRSA Fellow working in a corporate setting said, "Ultimately, they can decide not to take your counsel, but you have to make your view known and potentially what might unfold if they decide to take a different course."

Not all public relations professionals or scholars accept that public relations professionals have a role in ethics counseling. Some professionals insist ethics are better left to the legal department. They also argue that they lack the necessary access to provide ethics counsel (Bowen 2008). One Page Society member was reluctant to assume this role out of concern that what might be ethical might not be in the company's best interest. He gave the example of choosing to remain silent for legal reasons. He explained his support for a more limited role of providing ethics counsel:

My advice would be if you're in public relations, your reputation, risk is absolutely your domain. And reputation, risk and credibility and ethics go hand in hand, so it's all good. But don't fashion yourself into the chief ethics officer. I just don't think that's a good place to be…You're there to preserve the credibility of the organization and the senior executive team. Those are precious assets, but you're not the moral conscience of the organization. I just think those are different things.

Lack of access and training prompted Parsons (2008) to question public relations' role in ethics counseling. A PRSA Fellow acknowledged the limitations of access and influence:

The PR person can be the conscience, but are they listened to? Are they respected? Are they at the table? Those things are important as well because you can be doing everything right, but if nobody is listening to you, it really doesn't matter a whole lot. Except that you can sleep at night.

Chapters 2 and 3 provide guidance regarding how public relations professionals can become more influential, so that their colleagues seek their input and are more willing to listen to their counsel.

Regarding influence, Neill and Drumwright (2012) found public relations professionals who did not consider ethics counseling to be part of their job descriptions tended to be working in more entry-level positions and more focused on public relations tactics such as media relations and event planning. These same professionals, as one female government employee pointed out, did not have regular access to senior leadership and information:

> To be a good public relations professional, you need to have a lot of information from your organization…You really do need to have a seat at the table to listen and to hear what people are saying, how they're saying it, what information they're discussing. I couldn't be a good spokesperson if I didn't understand some of the internal discussions that are taking place, so I think that's very important…I think there have been some times where I haven't been in the room where I would have liked to have been in the room, because I think I would have had a deeper understanding of some of the issues or problems that I would then later be asked to speak about. (Neill and Drumwright 2012)

Despite the skepticism and resistance among some professionals, surveys with PRSA general membership and educators in the Public Relations Division of the Association for Education in Journalism and Mass Communication (AEJMC) found the majority (83 percent PRSA members and 96 percent educators) agree to strongly agree that practitioners should provide ethics counsel (Neill 2016a).

Public Relations' Role in Values Communication

Much of the discussion about public relations' ethics counseling role is focused on crisis prevention, but some scholars suggest professionals should be even more proactive as ethics advocates in their organizations (Men and Bowen 2017; Neill 2016b; Sison 2010). Marketing and human resources scholars have found that promoting an organization's core values can produce a distinct competitive advantage through employer-branding initiatives (Ambler and Barrow 1996; Foster, Punjaisri, and Cheng 2010; Lloyd 2002; Moroko and Uncles 2008; Vallaster and de Chernatony 2005). In a previous study, a female senior professional in the transportation industry included this role in her concept of an ethical conscience:

> For me, what that means is ensuring that the company, corporately, adheres to stated values, as well as ensuring that employees understand what those values are. And that involves working as a team also with HR to ensure that the follow through on hiring makes that clear to employees. (Neill and Drumwright 2012)

Through in-depth interviews with internal communication professionals, Neill (2016b) found that public relations professionals had a leadership role in creating strategic communication plans and distributing key messages about a company or organization's core values. They tended, however, to be less involved in employee recruitment and orientation, when employees are first introduced to the core values and/or ethics policies of an organization. Those communication efforts are led instead by human resources executives. Realizing the importance of delivering those messages earlier and more effectively, some public relations and marketing professionals reported that they were becoming more involved in creating promotional materials and videos for new employee orientation. More on this topic is covered in Chapter 8.

Summary

Many public relations professionals believe it is their responsibility to provide ethics counsel to senior leaders to help prevent crises. This role has been referred to as an ethical conscience, and it involves environmental scanning, or conducting research about the concerns of key stakeholders; and boundary spanning, which involves sharing those concerns with senior leadership.

Public relations professionals also proactively support ethics by promoting their company or organization's core values through routine communication efforts. This role of values communication is typically fulfilled in collaboration with human resource executives, who are responsible for communicating core values as part of employee recruitment and new employee orientation.

Questions to Ponder

1. How does your view of ethics in public relations compare to that of the senior executives quoted in this chapter?
2. Are there any employers that you believe do a good job of communicating and living their core values? If so, what are their best practices that you could follow?
3. What challenges might be associated with serving as a boundary spanner—someone with one foot in the organization while also representing the concerns of external stakeholders?

Ethical conscience as part of your role:
- Access to leadership
- Access to Information

CHAPTER 2

Influence and Power, Why Should I Care?

In Chapter 1, a senior public relations executive recalled the time when someone raised an ethical concern, only to see the advice ignored. Obviously this happens, probably more often than it should. So what can public relations professionals do to earn respect so that their counsel is valued? Prerequisites for serving as an ethical conscience include access to senior leaders to provide such counsel *and* the ability to actually influence them. However, 66 percent of PRSA members responding to a public relations ethics survey said they had faced the barriers of lack of access to leadership or information during their career (Neill 2016a).

Power has been defined as "getting things done, or getting others to do them" and influence is "the process through which power is actually used or realized" (Berger and Reber 2006, pp. 3–4; Pfeffer 1992). Power can be physical (coercive power), financial, or symbolic such as prestige (Mitchell, Agle, and Wood 1997). Power can be drawn from several sources, including individual characteristics, formal position or job titles, expertise, experience, relationships, and information (Berger and Reber 2006). Defining *influence* seems to be simpler. Through in-depth interviews with 65 public relations professionals, Berger and Reber (2006) found almost two-thirds of them defined influence as "holding a seat at the decision making table" (p. 17). Other definitions for influence included "having a voice" or "being listened to," and "the ability to convince others of your point of view" (Berger and Reber 2006, p. 18).

Neill (2015a) found that public relations executives tended to have more influence when issues were perceived as falling within their areas of expertise, such as crisis communication and reputation management. Other key factors impacting their degree of influence were the CEO's preference and the use of integrated decision teams, which tended to be larger and allowed for more diversity of perspectives based on both department and reporting levels (Neill 2015a). While not the case in every company, Neill (2012) found evidence of multiple integrated decision teams in one energy company. As evidence, the marketing council was comprised of some departments that might not be expected to weigh in on marketing issues:

> We have a marketing council...we don't have a vice president of marketing corporate...All the divisions have marketing VPs, and then we have other people that serve on this council...You'll have people in there from engineering. We do have marketing functions within the business units, so there would be marketing representatives from that group and public affairs always has at least one spot on there. You'll have some people from operations. (p. 57)

The same study revealed that public relations tended *not* to be influential or involved in strategic decisions when others did not follow proper protocol or issues were perceived as falling within another department's realm of expertise (Neill 2015a).

Organizational structure and reporting relationships also are essential factors that can enhance or hinder the ability of public relations executives to provide ethics counsel. As part of a large international study, Grunig, Grunig, and Dozier (2002) identified several, even ideal, structural characteristics of excellent public relations programs, such as departmental separation between public relations and marketing, a direct reporting relationship to senior management, and membership in the dominant coalition or C-Suite, "the group of individuals within the organization who have the power to determine its mission and goals" (pp. 141, 240–41). The term "C-Suite" is a reference to the titles of senior executives who have a coveted seat in the board room, such as the chief executive officer (CEO), chief financial officer (CFO), and chief marketing officer (CMO). Moss, Warnaby, and Newman (2000) found that public relations executives' access to the C-Suite is dependent on the personal credibility and standing of the individual professional, and others' perceptions of the quality of work and expertise of that executive.

While a C-Suite reporting structure might be ideal, it is not always reality. Survey research was conducted with members of the PRSA College of Fellows and Southern Public Relations Federation (SPRF) in May of 2017. When asked about their likelihood to be involved in high-level decision or policy-making meetings, the average response on a scale of 1 to 5 was 3.47 for SPRF members, indicating they were only somewhat likely to be involved; the average response for the College of Fellows was 4.0, indicating they were likely to be involved. These findings paralleled responses to another question about barriers. The majority of Fellows and SPRF members (59.7%, n = 43) indicated that yes, they have faced barriers when providing ethics counsel, and when responding via a checklist, the most common barriers selected were a hard-headed executive (n = 31), lack of access to meetings (n = 28), lack of influence (n = 19), and reporting relationship (n = 17). Bowen (2017) wrote about this first barrier in an article for *PR Week* regarding CEO *hubris*, which one male executive interviewed in 2012 found common in the corporate setting:

> I call it CEO disease and that is a disease born of inflated ego, oftentimes wealth, of stature or feeling of superior intelligence. When a person that oftentimes has ascended to the top levels of the company or organization feels like the rules just don't apply to them anymore. They apply to the little people and other people, but they don't apply to me...I worked for as I mentioned a CEO who said those rules just don't apply to me. That led to my resignation within two weeks. For a couple of reasons, one it was ethical abhorrent and illegal what he was doing and I was advising him not to do that anymore. I could go into details, but literally, legally it wasn't right...And that's when he literally leaned back in his chair and said, "Those rules just don't apply to me." (Neill and Drumwright 2012)

This same executive cited two additional barriers to ethics counsel, legal subterfuge and complicity:

> I've had to work in clearing news announcements or press responses and things oftentimes with in-house legal counsel. Not

that they're intentionally trying to lie or mislead, but they're literally trying to bury some stuff so much in legal mumbo jumbo that it's not clear or it's not entirely honest to me. Another, what I see...the third barrier is...complicity by others or others who are enablers. And that can come from any level in any organization where they're perfectly willing to go along with something that's ethically questionable to either keep their jobs, keep their paycheck or look good in the eyes of the boss. (Neill and Drumwright 2012)

These barriers are especially challenging and demonstrate a need for ethics training and strong mentors to help young professionals navigate these obstacles. Based on his experiences, this same male executive advised public relations professionals to set up expectations on the first day of the job. He recommended informing senior leaders that "you will be acting as the ethical conscience," "that you will in fact not always be that yes person, but will have to say no sometimes," and that "you can enlist others in power in your organization to back you up" (Neill and Drumwright 2012).

As for potential routes to access and information, Bowen (2009) found the most common path of access to senior leadership was a crisis situation; however, the access was only temporary, ending once the crisis was resolved. Other routes to access included ethical dilemma counseling, successful communication efforts that created credibility over time, media relations consulting on high-profile issues, and recognized leadership abilities. Many of these paths to influence, however, required years of service, and provided only limited access (Bowen 2009). One female senior executive working in higher education described it as a revolving door to access:

Our position within our organization still is not within the vice presidency like it is in some organizations, I guess that would give more direct access, but it has moved in and out of the presidential suite at different times, and there are certainly benefits to having open access there. So we just enjoy different reporting channels, different arrangements under different leaders. I think sometimes it comes down to the individual and how you're doing to make that reporting channel work. And unfortunately, you would like for that to be set in stone within the organization that you wouldn't have to continually fight those battles, but that's just been what I have perceived. (Neill and Drumwright 2012)

While most public relations research has focused on the C-Suite, more recently scholars pointed out that organizations actually have multiple coalitions including formal and informal committees formed on an *ad hoc* basis that meet at a range of venues including golf courses, coffee shops, fitness centers, and airports (Berger 2005; Neill 2014). Neill (2014) identified three distinct levels of formal coalitions as critical areas for public relations' participation: (1) the dominant coalition or C-Suite, (2) the leadership team for various company brands or divisions, and (3) executive-level committees. Some examples of executive-level committees that public relations executives reported serving on included the marketing council, diversity council, strategic spending team, and brand and reputation committee (Neill 2015a).

When public relations executives do not have access to executive-level meetings, some professionals, including this male professional working in higher education, contend their role is fire-fighting, rather than fire prevention:

They can't be excluded from the board room. They have to know what's going on. You can avoid a lot of messes if you engage upfront, rather than having to do PR battle, damage control later. If you're invited to the fire, why don't you invite them to the planning, then you can help avoid the fires. (Neill and Drumwright 2012)

A PRSA Fellow strongly urged public relations executives to fight for access, arguing that it might be the professional who pays the highest price without it:

When you do not even have the ability to offer solid counsel in the first place, there is a big problem. And as a practitioner maybe you can help change it and maybe you can't. And if you can't, maybe you need to think seriously about is this the right place for me to be at all. Because I could be the one shut out of what is going on and end up being the one thrown under the bus for it, and I have absolutely seen that happen and the individual didn't work hard enough to get that all important seat at the table and wasn't fully informed.

Social Influence

When public relations professionals do not have formal power and access to senior decision makers, social influence can be an alternative source of power. As Redmond and Trager (1998) wrote, "doing a good job is not enough. For your career to move forward, you have to be adept at social relationships, building alliances, and building trust among those above and below you in the hierarchy" (p. 154). Social influence refers to "a change in the belief, attitude or behavior of a person…which results from the action, or presence of another person" (Raven 1992, p. 218).

Power

French and Raven's (1959) five bases of power provide valuable insights for public relations professionals who desire more power and influence with senior executives, particularly in the context of ethics counsel. Their five sources of power are *reward, coercive, legitimate, referent*, and *expert/ informational* power. Reward and coercive power are simply the ability to administer rewards or punishments. Legitimate power is often acquired through social structure, age, or position. Tactics associated with legitimate power typically include direct orders and commands (Kahn, Wolfe, Quinn, Snoek, and Rosenthal 1964). Referent and expert power are most applicable for public relations professionals who do not report directly to the C-Suite (Berger and Reber 2006; Kahn et al. 1964). Referent power has been described as a feeling of oneness or identification with another; expert power is obtained through knowledge or ability in specialized areas (French and Raven 1959).

Effective tactics associated with referent and expert power include providing new information and reasoning to persuade the individual to accept a point of view (Kahn et al. 1964). Expert power also can be achieved through environmental scanning, a form of valued intelligence for organizational decision-making as discussed in Chapter 1, as well as other public relations' competencies, such as crisis communications and ghostwriting for executives (Neill 2015a). All of these tactics are ways of gaining more influence and access to senior leadership, and are crucial to effective public relations.

Consistent with referent and expert power, Holtzhausen and Voto (2002) found through a qualitative study that public relations professionals gained power through building relationships, acquiring expertise, and forming alliances. The in-depth interviews with senior executives and professionals for this study also revealed how critical relationships and alliances are to their ability to provide ethics counsel, so two full chapters (Chapters 3 and 5) are allotted to address these issues in more depth.

Additional insights on power and influence are found in Raven's (1992) power/interaction model of interpersonal influence. The process begins with (1) a purpose in influencing someone (e.g., attaining a goal, enhancing self-esteem, pressure from higher authorities), (2) an assessment of available power sources and preferences (e.g., legitimacy, expertise, referent power), (3) the use of self-presentation strategies referred to as "setting the stage," and (4) enacting the influence attempt.

Through an analysis of qualitative and survey data, some scholars discovered differences between men and women in their selection of power sources and the vocabulary used to describe their influence strategies. In a 2008 study, Aldoory and colleagues found that women listed the most valuable power sources as their level of reporting position, job performance, and access to key decision makers; men moved job performance to the top of the list and added expertise, data and research, and their personal knowledge of the business or organization. In addition, men were more likely to attempt to influence senior management through *direct* approaches such as "confront, combat, challenge or oppose;" women used less direct terms, such as "express, discussion, voice concerns" to describe their attempts to influence supervisors. Gender differences and power sources will be discussed more in Chapters 4 to 6.

Once the influencer selects the power source, he or she can then set the stage for influence through tactics such as providing background information and research, ingratiating oneself (i.e., compliments or flattery), and/or using self-promotion techniques such as displaying awards, or emphasizing commonality (Raven 1992). A senior public relations energy sector executive in a previous study by Neill (2012) described her use of one of these tactics, self-promotion by displaying pictures in her office of herself with elected officials as evidence of the important work she was doing:

> See the pictures—it's to prove we're—it's almost like here you're proving—they just know you're gone all the time, and they know you're out there doing something, but what is the value of what you're doing. This is like a congressman, the mayor...the former vice president of the United States, the governor. It's like we're really out there interfacing with these people. We're not just out there floating around. We're having an impact with regulators and elected officials. (p. 85)

Other related forms of self-promotion that executives can use include displaying awards, diplomas, and certifications in their offices. Another form of self-promotion is power by association. A PRSA Fellow told this story about accompanying a popular CEO on a plant visit after a merger to appear influential:

> When we were acquired, my CEO was considered a rock star, because (a) he had just sold his company for billions of dollars, so he was immediately very wealthy and he became the vice chairman. And I really intentionally did this—I went on a tour with him to meet with all these new businesses. So the first time they met me, I was right next to him. You know what I mean? So that helped me be perceived by the senior executives, so that when I became head of corporate communications for the larger company, that helped me have a rapport with the top executives right away.

Once the stage is set, then the communicator can select the appropriate influence strategy—reasoning, coalition building, invoking higher authority, and circumventing or going around the person or decision to achieve the result in an indirect manner (Redmond and Trager 1998). More details about influence strategies will provided in Chapters 4 to 6. Once the influence attempt is made, then the communicator must deal with the results. The influencer's "success or failure will lead to a reassessment of the available bases of power" and choice of future strategies (Raven 1992, p. 230).

A related concept worth consideration is *social capital theory,* which refers to "the sum of the actual and potential resources embedded within, available through, and derived from the network of relationships possessed by an individual or social unit" (Nahapiet and Ghoshal 1998, p. 243). Social capital delivers three major benefits: (1) access to information, (2) timeliness, or receiving information sooner than others, and (3) referrals by personal contacts who mention an associate's name at the right time and the right place, so that new opportunities develop (Burt 1992). Based on social capital theory, public relations professionals need a network of "contacts (a) established in places where useful bits of information are likely to air and (b) providing a reliable flow of information to and from those places" (Burt 1992, p. 15). Kennan and Hazelton (2006) discussed the importance of social capital in public relations and pointed out that professionals' knowledge of formal and informal networks impacts strategic decisions and the efficiency of communication, and for those reasons "knowing whom to talk with about what is important" (p. 284). In her study on social capital in public relations, Dodd (2012) found that due to public relations' boundary spanning role, they can serve as a "broker of social resources, filling a structural hole between the organization" and key publics. These social resources (i.e., connections, and their wealth, power, and reputation) are embedded in others with whom public relations professionals are in contact with, directly or indirectly. Dodd (2012) also suggested that social capital can be exchanged for tangible resources such as financial (e.g., departmental budget) or the achievement of goals and objectives.

One PRSA Fellow who had worked in government and legal settings made it a point to develop strong relationships with legal counsel as well as financial officers throughout her career:

I will tell you that is also part of my personal motivation to have good internal relationships with senior people who may be in a position to know and that's having a good relationship with legal counsel is super important, because you may not have access but they darn will and if they can bring you along great also. On the financial side, I find frequently that striking up sort of an internal dotted [informal] line relationship with either a peer or somebody above you in the financial corner of your organization's universe is great for both of you. They often feel a bit ill-equipped to deal with the communication portion because they are numbers people. And we feel the same way about what they do, so we can shore each other up and trade information and that's possibly where they can advocate for you. To say well "Why isn't [name of Fellow] here?" We need to have her here in this discussion.

This PRSA Fellow emphasized that these relationships often led to invitations to key meetings by allies who supported her inclusion. She said, "I do know I have been brought in through those people." She added that even when her position in the hierarchy did not provide access "allies advocate on my behalf...she really needs to be here."

Other Means of Gaining Influence

Senior executives can use other tactics to become more influential including conducting research, volunteering for tasks, and participating in cross-training sessions. Research, both primary and secondary, is consistent with environmental scanning, and can be used as a source of expert power (Kahn et al. 1964). As one corporate communications executive said:

You need to be aware of what's happening within your organization and outside of your organization. So I make it a practice myself to immerse myself in the trade magazines, so that I can keep up with what our competitors are doing, what major trends are ongoing in the business and oftentimes then sharing those news stories or those trends...with business heads...help them connect the dots, help them anticipate what might be coming down the road that we've got to prepare for. (Neill 2012, p. 83)

Conducting research prior to attending business meetings is also a smart practice. As this marketing executive advised:

Doing the research prior to going into a meeting...I believe is a very good strategy in a meeting that you're going to that you are not running, to research anything ahead of time that could come up or that you might be able to offer during the meeting itself and it helps lend to the conversation and it also helps...give you an extra air of credibility...because you have maybe more of a background of the issue than coming in blind. (Neill 2012, pp. 83–84)

While not everyone will be willing to adopt this next practice, Neill (2012) found one marketing executive had a reputation in her company for volunteering for tasks while attending meetings. One of her colleagues reflected on this pattern:

[Name of marketing director] tends to be a person who ends up with a lot of "to-dos" after a meeting, so does that make her more influential? I mean it's nice to have a person who says, "Ok, I'll take that. I'll do that. I'll take that." So she, I would say thinking about all those planning meetings...she probably took the lion's share of a lot of the to-dos away from those meetings, which is great...that probably makes her a little more influential...then she's reporting back..."Here's what I did on this. Here's what I did on that"...So I think there's a correlation there between somebody volunteering to take that extra work on and then having some influence. (Neill 2012, p. 84)

Neill (2012) also found that in one energy company, cross-training and in-depth knowledge of the business were highly valued. For those reasons, employees tended to move laterally in the company to learn about the various divisions before being promoted to more senior positions. As one public affairs executive said:

I've had a lot of experiences and a lot of different jobs, which really helped train me to have a good understanding of the entire company…So I always tell new employees coming in—everybody feels like they have to go straight up, but sometimes it's good to go sideways and learn all that you can, so that you're more valuable. (Neill 2012, p. 85)

Summary

Effective public relations management requires professionals to seek power and influence. Public relations professionals do not always report directly to the C-Suite in their companies and organizations. There are other ways, however, for them to be influential. As they build a reputation for success through communication campaigns, media relations, and crisis communication, they gain influence. Other ways to become influential include building relationships with experts in other departments such as legal and finance, conducting research in order to have solid evidence to support your counsel, and using self-promotion tactics. On the opposite side of the spectrum, public relations professionals who are uninvolved and not informed regarding management decisions, and therefore not influential, could become the scapegoat when things go south during a crisis situation.

Questions to Ponder

1. What are some of the barriers public relations professionals face in their efforts to provide ethics counsel and how can they overcome them?
2. What are some techniques that public relations professionals can use to become more influential?
3. Can you think of any examples of effective tactics for "setting the stage" for influence that you have witnessed? Why do you think these approaches were effective?

CHAPTER 3

Don't Overlook Your Office Neighbors: Why You Need to Focus on Building Internal Relationships

It is not given that public relations professionals will embrace the role of ethical conscience. Some believe it is too big a job for one person (St. John III and Pearson 2016). We agree. It is too big a job for one person; many of those interviewed concurred. That is why many of the personal accounts that public relations professionals tell about raising ethical concerns involve recruiting allies or forming coalitions, as there is power in numbers. It is simply a matter of building and maintaining relationships, an accepted and expected role for public relations professionals.

Coalitions are "any subset of a group that pools its resources or unites as a single voice to determine a decision for the entire group" (Murnighan and Brass 1991, p. 285), but the difficulty in studying coalitions is the secrecy which can surround their activities. Berger and Reber (2006) suggested that coalitions meet both formally—scheduled meetings at designated sites with an agenda—and informally, impromptu meetings in airplanes, golf courses, hallways, parking lots, or via video conferences. Similarly, Neill (2014) found informal meetings often occurred in coffee shops, fitness centers, electronically through text messages, and impromptu stops by a colleague's office.

In their research, Eisenhardt and Bourgeois (1988) found that coalitions did not necessarily form based on agreement on specific issues, but around factors such as age, proximity of offices, similar job titles, and prior work experiences together. Scott (1981) noted that "coalition members seek out other groups whose interests are similar as allies, and they negotiate with groups whose interests are divergent but whose par-ticipation is necessary" (p. 264). The invitations to participate in these informal coalitions are often based on interpersonal relationships. So, before recruiting allies and forming coalitions, public relations profes-sionals need to form trusting relationships with their colleagues in other departments throughout the company or organization. As a Page Society member explained:

> I had a relationship with them previously....it really came down to know you, like you, trust you. You've worked with them, you've seen them in different situations, you knew how the other responded, you'd seen them in action, so you knew what their character was or you knew that they cared about this type of issue or that they had a strong sense of right or wrong.

A PRSA Fellow emphasized how critical relationships are to effective public relations and also described the investment that it requires:

> You can't always go it alone. You can't do that...so you need to recruit allies by appealing to their sense of decency and honesty, and...[if] management hears more than one voice with a con-vincible argument, you know with any luck they're going to acqui-esce and listen. It is our stock in trade...It's relationship building and it's not a momentary event. It's one that's done over time by building allies, helping them understand the value you bring to the table, to being open and honest with them. And always help-ing out whenever somebody needs help and over time that builds tremendous trust, so once you have built that trust you know it doesn't easily fall apart unless you've done something unethical or dishonest or hurtful. And so my philosophy in my career has always been to build allies before you need them.

This PRSA Fellow provided several recommendations regarding how to build relationships with your coworkers:

> You have to reach out to people and have the genuine interest of who they are, what their background is, what their expertise is.

I think asking for help in learning about what they do can be a great way to open doors. I think finding things that you have in common are also very positive ways to build a relationship. I think being open to having different kinds of conversations and really making yourself accessible.

A Page Society member took another approach to relationship building, asking colleagues for their advice:

I found over time that the best way I had to build trust was to consult with my peers when I had a decision to make and ask for their help. When you ask for someone's help, it's the easiest way to make a friend, because they feel like you need them and that you are intensely interested in their point of view. And so that was a hard lesson for me to learn, but when I did finally learn it, and get really good at it, I found it was highly effective.

Another PRSA Fellow took a proactive and personal approach to building relationships:

I started the day I went to work or the day they went to work, whichever came first or last, so...they knew I was interested in them, I visited with them, I heard what they had to say, so I would be on a relationship. Like to see all the pictures of their kids, I went to see their kids when they were born, I took them a little potluck...I just worked the relationship, which is what we're all about.

At the same time, as this senior executive for a Fortune 500 company and member of the Arthur W. Page Society stressed, it is important to look for specific characteristics among allies:

I found like-minded individuals who are interested in ensuring that the culture and the way we behave at [name of employer] continued to be something that's special and unique and something that we would never ever allow to be sacrificed. And we have a very loose, informal, yet very well-identified coalition of people who bonded and said, regardless of what role we serve inside of the company, and regardless of who we work for, we will always ensure that we speak up and challenge and counsel to ensure that [name of employer] continues to always do the right thing for our members and our employees.

While this may sound time consuming and even disruptive to a normal routine, in reality many of these relationships are built while working together on cross-departmental projects for the company or organization. As a PRSA Fellow explained, building these alliances should be part of the routine:

> It's part of our job anyway to understand this business and learning about their challenges they face, the issues they face, the triumphs that they experience. I think public relations has a great opportunity to do that because we can be champions for people. We can shine a bright light on the good work the different parts of an organization do, so we're natural allies and so when we act as allies in that way, we actually build trust. And so having that kind of curious mind—explain that to me, help me understand it. I want to be able to explain that to other people is generally trust building. We have to take the time to do that, and then when people feel like you understand their business…then the relationship just gets stronger.

Some of the relationship building occurs through formal and officially sanctioned business activity. While the traditional focus in public relations has been gaining access to the C-Suite, Berger (2005) discussed the importance of a new paradigm that focuses on *multiple* coalitions such as crisis and safety committees and public affairs management teams. Similarly, in an in-depth study of four companies, Neill (2014) found public relations executives were highly involved in formal leadership teams at the division level, as well as executive-level committees—such as a strategic spending team and a brand and reputation committee. She also discovered that public relations executives often chose to collaborate with those working in similar communication functions such as investor relations, marketing, and government affairs (Neill 2014). They also tended to communicate with those whose offices were next door and those with shared experiences, such as attending the same university. One corporate communications officer maintained that there is common ground to be found, if you look for it:

> We office right next to each other. And because IR [investor relations] and PR are linked, and so there's this constant back and forth between us on how to position an issue and how to explain it, what to include in a news release versus what to include in a conference call, etc. So there's lots of—it's partnering and teaming. (Neill 2014, p. 601)

Some of these relationships, as one senior vice president of investor relations explained, are built through informal activities, whether a casual stop by a colleague's office, a morning chat at the coffee shop, or going for a walk or run with a colleague:

> An example of that is when [SVP of corporate communications] and I would sit down over Starbucks at 7 in the morning and just say, "Hey what's going on in your world today? What are you expecting?" And so then issues would come up and we would bounce ideas off of each other, and I always found that that was a really good way to start the day. (Neill 2014, p. 603)

At one Fortune 500 energy company, managers deliberately focused on having their public affairs employees learn the business and meet their colleagues in other departments, which this division president believed paid big dividends:

> If you come to work with us in public affairs, we take the first year with you and we just put you through the ringer. You've got work boots; you're going to have steel toe boots; you're going to have a hard hat. You're going to be in the field...so that when you're standing in front of a camera, and someone sticks a mic in front of you...you don't do this—"uh, uh." (Neill 2012, pp. 84–85)

Similarly, a Page Society member decided to work behind the counter of their restaurants to better understand the concerns of employees and customers. She said, "I think it's really incumbent upon us to get out there and get out from behind our desks and spend as much time with colleagues and customers and stakeholders as possible."

One PRSA Fellow made it a priority to develop strong relationships with senior finance and legal officers:

> The person I frequently go to is whoever the top financial reporting person is whether it is the chief operating officer [COO], or CFO…I frequently like to get the money analytical budget person on board because they come at things from a very different perspective and frequently things do involve money issues so it has informed me about things I don't know. And I don't want to get broadsided at a big meeting. I tend to try to develop very good relationships with people in those areas, because it is so as far afield from what I do…I've worked in politics a lot. You want to count up the votes before you get in there…Often I learn about red flags I did not know about and shift my own thinking.

A member of the Page Society said this approach is consistent with the Japanese consensus-building principle known as *nemawashi*. Public relations executives need to privately meet with other senior executives to hear their concerns and craft a solution that would be mutually beneficial, just as they would with external stakeholders. Legal counselors are a good example. While some public relations professionals considered legal an adversary, others see them as key collaborators. As a former Page Society member said, "It used to be that PR and legal were always at odds. Most senior executives know that legal is your best friend." A PRSA Fellow also said she actively seeks out legal as an ally:

> I always gravitated to working with legal counsel. Their interests are extremely important and in a lot of ways I think they're as close to public relations practitioners as I am going to get inside an organization and I just plain like lawyers. I always wanted to work with them and make sure they were an ally and not an

adversary. Frequently our interests clashed. And if we could work it out among ourselves first, it often made it so much easier to go after these issues on a bigger scale when the boss has to make the decision.

While it is always important for public relations professionals to understand the business and interests of other departments, they also need to make it a priority to educate their colleagues on the value of public relations. As a public affairs director at an energy company said:

> You can't force people to think of you first. So you have to pro-actively go in and be willing to assist them and just be there for them and show them how helpful you can be to them. I see a lot of public relations people that are sort of snobbish that…act like oh, "I'm the big TV guy…and I don't have time for you people." We try to be the opposite, and we try to go in and show them our interest by going to them…"How can I be of help to you? What can we do? What are your issues? What are your problems? How can I help you with them?" (Neill 2014, p. 603)

Organizational Factors Impacting Collaboration

Relationship building can produce true collaboration that leads to the exchange of information, sharing of ideas and resources, and responsiveness to others' needs, as well as consensus building (Lee, Jares, and Heath 1999), but in reality, too many organizations still operate in functional silos. In those situations, departments do not communicate with each other. They often operate without awareness of what is happening in other parts of the organization. When this happens, it can lead to miscommunication, distrust, duplication of services, turf battles, and a focus on protecting a department's domain and budget (Kitchen, Spickett-Jones, and Grimes 2007; Neill 2015b; Ots and Nyilasy 2015). Collaboration and functional silos can both be considered outcomes of an organization's climate, culture, policies, and procedures, and also can impact ethical decision-making (Bowen 2004; McDonald and Nijhof 1999; Neill and Schauster 2015).

An ethical climate refers to an organization's behavioral norms, role models, and historical anecdotes about times when the company chose to do the right thing (Cohen 1993). An organization's culture includes its stated and practiced core values, which are "deeply ingrained principles that guide all of a company's actions" and serve as "cultural cornerstones" (Lencioni 2002, p. 6). As an illustration of these principles in practice, a chief marketing officer for a nonprofit organization described how they shifted their culture from silos to a more collaborative environment.

> The way we were structured before—and this went all the way down to how employees were annually reviewed—if you ran a specific development program…and your revenue goal was $30 million, that's what you focused on. And so you acted like that, which caused you to work in a silo versus now we value collaboration and working without silos and being innovative. And so you see a lot of cross functional teams. A lot less about who's owning it. (Neill 2016b, p. 12)

A PRSA Fellow held face-to-face meetings to overcome functional silos:

> I took the time to sit down with each department, with each department head and work through their, first of all what are they all about, what they are trying to accomplish, what's their business plan look like in support of the greater organization, and how can I and my team help that…the departments get very siloed, and in this case the silos were pretty high and pretty thick in terms of the walls and…busting silos is very important to making things work internally sometimes, if not oftentimes. And so it was necessary to make sure that everyone could start to see the connections between what they were doing and what others were doing in the organization and how important it was for them to all have a consistent direction with one another.

Some communication executives also discussed how structural changes may be necessary to combat functional silos that exist even within the communication function:

We have a new chief communications officer and that's a new role that we didn't have until about the last year. And that person is over external, internal, our shows and events team, as well as our executive communications team. So before that, we…all operated in our siloed organizations. So the fact that we have one SVP who is driving the strategy and the operations for all of those functions, is pretty telling that we're really leaning into more integrated communications approach. (Neill and Jiang 2017, p. 7)

These personal accounts provide evidence that collaboration is necessary for ethical decision-making in a company or organization. Understanding a company or organization's management style is also important for public relations executives when trying to build relationships and foster collaboration. Companies and organizations that illustrate McGregor's (1960) *Theory Y* (participatory) management style use decentralized management, allow for autonomy in decision-making, and use cross-departmental teams to solve problems (Bowen 2004; Redmond and Trager 1998). These factors empower public relations executives to assume an all-important role, that of a *strategic adviser*. By contrast, *Theory X* (authoritarian) management has been described as the "command and control approach," based on the notion that employees need to be "coerced, controlled, directed, threatened with punishment" in order to achieve company objectives (McGregor 1960, as cited in Redmond and Trager 1998, p. 43). The authoritarian leadership style uses top-down decision-making and leads to a greater power-distance relationship between the leadership and employees (Bowen 2004; Redmond and Trager 1998). In addition, formal authority and position in the organizational chart are prioritized over expertise when determining committee assignments or composition of leadership teams (Bunderson 2003); so, if public relations executives are positioned lower in the hierarchy, they have less opportunity to provide strategic counsel.

As evidence of a participative culture, a division president for an energy company said, "I tend to value the people far above what title or department they come from; you know, what's their ability to contribute?" As further support for a de-emphasis on formal titles and roles, he described how an engineer was leading a philanthropy effort in the company: "Look everybody has an opinion…We have a public affairs effort right now that's going to be around this year's election. But it's… helping the…food bank. And the guy that's leading it is an engineer. Perfect example of it." (Neill 2012, p. 58)

A participative culture allows public relations executives to serve as internal boundary spanners by linking people and coordinating activities, as well as filtering and transferring information across departments and up and down the hierarchy (Jemison 1984; Miles 1976; Neill 2014). As evidence of this role, Neill (2014) found public relations executives who would share updates during their departmental meetings with colleagues who were serving in leadership roles across the corporation, allowing issues to be examined from a companywide perspective. It was through this wider lens that public relations executives detected proposed actions that were problematic and needed to be addressed. More importantly, this intelligence enabled them to provide valuable strategic counsel.

Summary

The strategy of building relationships across an organization is critical to effective and strategic public relations generally and a prerequisite to serve as an ethical conscience. Strong relationships can lead to collaboration and create an environment that encourages ethical deliberation and decision-making. However, an organization's culture and climate can serve as barriers to collaboration and ethics counseling. More specifically, functional silos may make it difficult to gather information and build trust among colleagues in other departments. Face-to-face meetings with department heads are one way to overcome this barrier.

Questions to Ponder

1. Why is it important for public relations professionals to build relationships with colleagues in other departments?
2. Based on the specific accounts in this chapter, what are some of the best approaches for building relationships with colleagues in other disciplines?
3. What are some of the organizational barriers that can prevent internal departments from collaborating with each other?

CHAPTER 4

Influence Strategies Senior Pros Prefer to Use

One of the best ways to learn how to effectively provide ethics counsel is to talk to those who have actually done so, and learn from their successes and mistakes. With that goal in mind, in-depth interviews were conducted with 34 members of the PRSA College of Fellows, 21 members of the Arthur W. Page Society, and members of the PRSA College of Fellows and the Southern Public Relations Federation (SPRF) were invited to participate in an online survey. Using the influence tactics framework developed by Berger and Reber (2006), interviewees and survey participants were asked which of the Alpha/Sanctioned tactics and Omega/Unsanctioned tactics they had employed.[1] Some of the most common Alpha tactics include rational approaches such as using research and case studies, recruiting allies and forming coalitions, exerting pressure by being persistent and assertive, and employing emotional and legitimacy appeals (Berger and Reber 2006). Omega tactics involve leaking information to external stakeholders, planting rumors, sabotaging implementation of a decision, and serving as a whistleblower (Berger and Reber 2006). During the in-depth interviews, some senior executives discussed additional tactics they used, such as asking probing questions, presenting alternative solutions or creating various scenarios for their bosses to consider, and applying the "headline test," which involves having senior leaders consider potential media coverage of their decision. *The choice of influence tactics varies by both experience and gender.*

---

 [1] Alpha tactics are those that are socially accepted and widely used. Omega tactics tend to be used as a last resort when Alpha tactics are not successful in achieving desired results.

Comparing the survey results from the PRSA College of Fellows and the general membership of SPRF (see Appendix A), the average age of the respondent sample was 51, with participants ranging in age from 20 to 79. The average years of experience in public relations for the SPRF sample were 16 years and 37 years for the College of Fellows. When asked about the influence strategies and tactics the professionals actually used, the top choice for the combined sample was apparent with almost 81 percent of the professionals choosing the tactic of asking questions, listening and engaging in dialogue. One male PRSA Fellow had used this approach successfully:

> It's engaging in dialogue…you have to start by asking the person… first, what do you think? Or where do you want to go? Where do you want to be or what is it that is bothering you? So if you get a baseline and then you understand the differences between your-self and that person or management…and you know what you have to bridge. So it gives you…a work plan as to how to get to a successful point.

Almost three-fourths of the respondents (72%) chose a direct approach as their second choice. A male PRSA Fellow described the direct approach this way: "Not looking the other way, challenging people. Suggesting that maybe something that they were thinking about doing might be unethical." He later added, "I mean basically if I thought it was wrong I'd go to the CEO and tell them it is wrong. I don't need supporters." The senior executives interviewed appeared to choose a direct approach when they found a request to be highly objectionable. One male PRSA Fellow recalled an offer by a lobbyist to blackmail a politician:

> There was a lobbying firm involved that was hired locally, and we met in Washington with our corporate lobbying firm. And the local lobbying firm had put a brown envelope on the table, and said, "Well, if things get really tough, we have some not so nice information on this local official"…And I said, "No…you can take that off the table. We're not going to even open that and go there."

A female PRSA Fellow remembered the time she had to take strong stance with an influential donor who wanted to threaten a media organization if it did not agree to sponsor a nonprofit fundraiser:

> I just looked at the guy and I said, "You know here's the deal. If you want to call the TV station and do that, I think that's totally up to you. I think it's unethical...And no, I will not call the TV station and tell them...this donor's going to yank all this advertising from you unless you do this. That's called blackmail and coercion and that's illegal, and I'm not going to do it. So if that's a decision you want to make, feel free to make that decision and... my involvement here is complete...no, I will not compromise my integrity and character"...So I got up and left the meeting.

Contrasting responses between PRSA Fellows and SPRF general membership, differences were found in the selection of top influence strategies. Overwhelmingly, the majority of PRSA Fellows (91%) selected the tactic of asking questions, listening and engaging in dialogue as their top tactic, and the majority of SPRF members (72%) selected it as their top tactic as well. PRSA Fellows (85%) chose legitimacy appeals as their second go-to influence strategy, 82 percent preferred personal experiences next, and 79 percent equally supported the strategies of raising the concerns of stakeholders and the direct approach (see Table 4.1). The second choice for SPRF members was a direct approach (67%), followed by use of scenarios/alternatives/solutions (62%), raising the concerns of stakeholders (56%), and legitimacy appeals and personal experiences (each 51%).

Table 4.1 Ranking of top influence strategies

Strategies	College of Fellows	SPRF
Asking questions/listening/dialogue	1	1
Legitimacy appeals	2	5/6 (tie)
Personal experiences	3	5/6 (tie)
Direct approach	4/5 (tie)	2
Raise concerns of stakeholders	4/5 (tie)	4
Use of scenarios/alternatives/solutions	6	3

Based on the in-depth interviews, the most common influence strategies preferred by members of the Page Society were personal experiences and legitimacy appeals, followed by allies and case studies (see Appendix D). The PRSA Fellows listed case studies first, followed by legitimacy appeals, allies, and research (see Appendix C). One of the key differences appears to be the priority placed on research. Some Page Society members said they were less likely to use research based on timing and lack of funding; however, other Page Society members were able to describe specific times when research played a central role in their counsel. As one Page Society member explained:

> I went from an organization where we spent no money on research—it costs money sometimes, generally, to the point that I get people to buy into it that can immediately spend 2% of what this program is costing to do research to prove its effectiveness. I like to do that research in advance of it, not after, to see whether or not it worked. I want to make sure that what we're planning works...And you need a couple of wins in that space, and not costing too much money and you win people over.

Both groups, the PRSA Fellows and Page Society, have extensive experience in public relations and can easily draw upon their personal experiences when providing ethics counsel. One Page Society member said she uses storytelling as a means of sharing personal experiences:

> I always like to say, "Well, in my experience, let me tell you a story about this, and you would think this wouldn't be a big deal, but let me tell you how it escalated, and what we had to do to correct it." So yeah, whenever possible personal stories are hugely impactful when it comes to persuasion.

In previous studies, scholars found that rational persuasion (e.g., use of data, case studies, and laws) was the most common influence technique public relations professionals reported using, followed by coalition-building, then using pressure or assertiveness (Berger and Reber 2006; O'Neil 2003). Rational persuasion would be consistent with legitimacy appeals, which was the second most common influence tactic used by PRSA Fellows and was among the two top tactics preferred by Page Society members. Legitimacy appeals are arguments based on what is legal or ethical, and can involve calling attention to the organization's core values. Berger and Reber (2006) labeled these approaches as structural resources, pointing out that they can be drawn from an organization's policies and procedures. A female PRSA Fellow said structural resources were part of her ethical toolkit:

> I've also used mission, vision, those points in discussions where I'll say…well, Ok, if we do x, y, z, I don't think that's in keeping with our mission, vision, values. I think that those…statements that a company has already adopted can be extremely effective and oftentimes more effective than saying, "I just don't think that's ethical." If you can say that our value is to always be transparent and does this really meet those values, I think it's an even stronger statement…because you're tying it back to something that a company has already decided they believe in.

A member of the Page Society said his approach involved posing a simple question due to their strong ethical culture when faced with a potential security breach:

> I was new enough to ask this sort of dumb/bold question— what would our founder do? And I work for a company where our founder is still active in the business. And then I said, "Well, what would he do?" And both the head of sales and the head of the enterprise looked at me and said, "Yeah, you're right." And we made the decision in about 10 seconds. And we went on and we notified all those people [customers].

Another female PRSA Fellow remembered using a legitimacy appeal during an internal debate following a traffic accident involving a contractor the company had hired that resulted in the death of a youth. She advocated for the company to offer condolences to the grieving family:

I had a conversation about it and the other execs about what our roles should be in reaching out to the family of the dead man, and most advised against it. In fact, every executive advised against it. I had a private conversation with our president and said, "You know this is a tough issue, and there's no right answer here. Here are the pros and cons of calling this grieving mother and your legal counsel doesn't think it's a good idea, but that's not who you are. You care about people and our company cares about people and it seemed consistent with who you and the way that we define ourselves as a company that we would acknowledge this woman's grief." And so it was a very difficult call. He didn't have a lot of support. And in the end, he decided that yes that his instinct that his belief as a human being and a leader of the company that obviously had some connection to the event that he would call and talk to this mother.

Based on the depth of their experience, it is no surprise that the PRSA Fellows were more likely than the general membership of SPRF, a regional professional association, to draw upon their personal experiences when providing ethics counsel. Experience has been classified as an individual resource, based on skills and personal characteristics such as intelligence, integrity, and vision (Berger and Reber 2006). Other examples of individual influence resources include expertise, performance, and knowledge of the organization. A male PRSA Fellow found his personal experiences as invaluable:

In terms of personal experience, I think you after being in the business for so many years, it's sort of like Malcolm Gladwell's theory of 10,000 experiences and pretty soon you do all of your own sets of case studies and personal research.

That is exactly what one Page Society member said he did was to create his own library of case studies:

I would go out in search of case studies wherever I could. And I often wrote them, meaning I wrote about a company having an experience so...you write a concise...here's the issue they faced that's similar to ours. Here's how they addressed it, and here's what they would have done differently. And the great thing about corporations and the agency people I've worked with, they're very sharing and open. They don't necessarily want these things published. But they're willing to share personal experiences including failures.

As expected, Omega/Unsanctioned tactics, such as leaking information externally or serving as a whistleblower, were less likely to be used by the PRSA Fellows or SPRF members. A few instances, however, were reported during in-depth interviews and those accounts will be discussed in Chapter 6.

Gender Differences Regarding Influence Strategies

Gender differences also were examined in choice of influence strategies reported by PRSA Fellows and Page Society members during the in-depth interviews (see Appendix B). Analysis found men preferred to use (1) case studies, (2) legitimacy appeals, (3/4) allies and personal experiences (5) research, and (6) pressure (see Table 4.2). The women equally preferred (1/2/3) legitimacy appeals, allies and pressure, followed by (4) personal experiences, and (5/6) case studies and research.

Table 4.2 *Ranking of influence tactics by gender*

Influence tactic	Men	Women
Case studies	1	5/6 (tie)
Legitimacy appeals	2	1/2/3 (tie)
Allies	3/4 (tie)	1/2/3 (tie)
Personal experiences	3/4 (tie)	4
Research	5	5/6 (tie)
Pressure	6	1/2/3 (tie)

One male PRSA Fellow provided his own description of these various approaches:

If you can bring some sort of personal perspective to it that helps, but barring that I think it helps clients hear other companies have faced the same circumstance or dealt with the same ethical issue, and…this is how they handled it and this is how they dealt with it. This is what we recommended they do and they came through the other side Ok. So I'd say anytime there's a personal experience that you can add to that the better, but I would say…case studies are probably the most effective with clients that I work with and then if there's skepticism, then research certainly helps maybe seal the deal or give them further comfort that Ok this is…what's happening throughout the industry.

Research and case studies would be examples of informational resources (Berger and Reber 2006). A female PRSA Fellow described exactly how to use case studies in a less confrontational manner:

And I think case studies provide a way for you to say, "Hey, I have a concern about this and I started looking into it. And this company I think maybe it was doing something similar." And almost asking the other person to read the case study and then to tell me how they feel. Because I think that a lot of times you can talk, talk, talk, talk, but if you can show and then wait and then listen, the other person or the other party will see what it is that you're going for and then it's their own idea to change to a more ethical tactic rather than you having to push it on them.

Women senior executives tend to use different influence strategies than men, specifically allies and pressure. One reason women might be more likely to recruit allies is they tend to be outnumbered by men in the boardroom, as reported by one female PRSA Fellow working in education, "I'm the person who came up where I would be the only woman on the leadership team." A member of the Page Society shared a similar experience and described how challenging that can be:

Often I'm the only woman in the room, and…it's high stakes and high pressure, and so a lot of times the men will scream, yell, curse, pace. And to have your voice heard, a lot of times, I will stand up and walk like kind of in front of the room. I just say listen, and so I will have to definitely be more assertive than I typically would be to get attention and get people to focus... But it's usually in a pretty calm demeanor, but a pretty assertive demeanor as well..."Listen, other companies have faced this in the past. It's not the end of the world. Here's what I recommend." And it usually can get people...to refocus.

Allies and coalitions are examples of what Berger and Reber (2006) called relational influence resources, which will be discussed in more detail in Chapter 5. It is important to note that many of the women interviewed said they used pressure in connection with allies or other coalition members, so the two techniques, while separate tactics, tend to be related. A female PRSA Fellow said there is strength in numbers:

I think when you have more than one person saying the same thing it's helpful. So it wasn't like I really had to really recruit them. I just had to make them aware of what was happening. And so I think going in force can help your case. Sometimes it can backfire...you know if somebody wants to kill the messenger. But most of the time if you hear something from one person, you'd [think] like yeah, that might be true, but if several people come to you with the same messaging, I think you take notice.

Another female PRSA Fellow described a situation involving a controversial recommendation from engineers unfamiliar with the local community as an example of allies effectively applying pressure:

When they presented it to us, we all said, "This cannot happen. You will decimate a culture if you do this"...And that was very emotional for us, because these were people that we knew. These were people that we had been in their homes. We had had meals with their families. We had talked with them about being a very responsible developer and being honest...We will not do this moving forward.

An additional insight was discovered from observing the specific language men and women used to describe their influence strategies and tactics in practice. Previous researchers found men were more likely to attempt to influence senior management through direct approaches such as "confront, combat, challenge or oppose" while women used terms such as "express, discussion, voice concerns" to describe their attempts to influence supervisors (Aldoory et al. 2008). In this study, the male senior executives interviewed used descriptions such as ask questions, discuss or listen; present, share alternatives and solutions; or recommend and counsel. A few men also used more confrontational descriptions, such as "we're not going to do that," "that's not how we operate," "pushed hard," "firm not wavering," and "tell them it's wrong." Women senior executives tended to describe their attempts in less confrontational terms such as discuss/listen/dialogue; and recommended, suggested, counseled, and advised. However, a few of the women used more direct approaches such as coming "down fairly hard" on a position, making it very clear, being straightforward, being forceful, "we absolutely put our foot down," or urging clients to "tell me the truth now." Again, some of those more confrontational approaches discussed by women were in the context of joint efforts with allies or coalition members. Specific examples regarding how to recruit allies and coalition members are discussed in Chapter 5.

Other Approaches to Ethics Counsel

When confrontation or pressure has not been effective or needs to be avoided, public relations executives can be quite resourceful when identifying ways to approach more senior executives. One method mentioned is the so-called "headline test" (Neill and Drumwright 2012), which asks senior executives to consider the potential media consequences of their decisions. An Australian female public relations executive cited in a previous study described the technique:

It's like what do you want the story to be? What's the good story that you can imagine and the bad story you can imagine. I don't have to explain it there for them now. They can sit there and think about it. It could go this way. Is that the headline? (Neill and Drumwright 2012, p. 227)

A related approach, which a female PRSA Fellow found effective, involved having senior leaders consider potential consequences through the use of scenarios and risk assessment:

> It's important to present a number of scenarios, and show the level of risks associated with which one rather than come and say, "This is wrong; we've got to do it this way." Rather than just a one option approach, say here's option A, here's option B, and here's option C, and here are the risks associated with each one. And you know option C is going to be your most ethical approach, fewer legal risks, etc. And I think by painting that picture of I would say the spectrum of risks, you're not telling the CEO or the C-Suite what to do, but you're letting them understand the risks and providing recommendations. But it's ultimately their decision.

A male public relations executive working in education shared another example of providing alternatives:

> I was given basically a script for a speech the superintendent was going to read related to the action we were taking, and I felt like the action we were taking was purely politically driven by forces in the community and wasn't really necessarily the will of our people or the right thing to do in the situation we were in and so I… did my speech writing job on the one I was given, but also wrote a second version that I felt like was more what we should do and turned those back in and said please take a look at the second version, and the second version is what was done and that was after no other leadership discussion beyond just me offering that and then that's what was done. (Neill and Drumwright 2012)

Another common approach used by public relations executives is raising an ethical concern from the perspective of key stakeholders. A male PRSA Fellow described the appeal he used based on the concerns of local community members.

> And the neighborhood was low socioeconomic, and…they were already extremely upset by changes the company had made,

which were very courteous, but not delivered in a kind way. It's kind of like take it or leave it. And we had to explain to them this is how these people feel. It's not that you were wrong. You did the right things. But it's the way it was delivered...And once we explained that to this vice president, he said, "Oh my gosh, I didn't think of it that way."...When the whole thing was said and done...the group threw a thank you party for the company. It was a community block party.

Raising concerns from the perspective of stakeholders can involve assuming the role of devil's advocate or loyal opposition. Shahinpoor and Matt (2007) pointed out that the person taking on this role does not have to disclose his or her personal views, and does not necessarily have to agree with the views of these stakeholders. A male public relations professional working in education used this tactic when dealing with a potential breach in computer security:

I think looking at it from the student [perspective] and the repercussions of that decision, looking at it from the parents and trying to anticipate questions or concerns that parents would have and making sure that we were being informative and fully disclosing what we should to parents as well. And so I think a lot of it has to do with examining the decision from the context of the individuals that will be affected by that decision. Again, it's knowing your audience and it's understanding what their needs, what their expectations are going to be. (Neill and Drumwright 2012)

No one approach is perfect for every scenario, and public relations executives choose the method that fits their personality style and the specific circumstances. One female PRSA Fellow said it also was important to know your audience:

I could use a chapter from a book with an HR business partner, because I knew she was a little more academic and intellectual, and she would see the picture that I was seeing. Case studies have been helpful in again situations like I was describing when I was kind of dividing and conquering another higher level of leadership was what helped me to convince the woman who headed up a global organization. I shared case studies/articles that talked about communicating effectiveness and again, the research in terms of employees. ...I think for me, it's been knowing who is that I'm trying to influence, what's going to resonate with them, and what's not going to resonate with them.

One Page Society member said he draws from his personal faith when counseling others:

Most of the time, I'm trying to work Biblical principles into what I'm actually doing, and...so many times, where I'll go is Biblical principles minus the chapter and verse, because in many cases, in most cases, I've found that works really well, because...it underpins the legal system, because it underpins so many other systems within our culture, that's always been incredibly helpful. And yeah, it's literally a matter of kind of stripping out the chapter and verse.

As an example of this approach, he added: "Vision being the easiest—without a vision the people perish."

Approaches to Avoid

Knowing what *not* to do can often be as important as knowing what works. While the senior executives discussed their preferred approaches, they also provided advice regarding how not to confront senior executives. A male senior executive working in education provided this advice regarding confronting a CEO: "You don't want to tell them they're wrong. You want to give them the advice in a way that they can handle it...So you have to sort of nuance it." (Neill and Drumwright 2012)

A female PRSA Fellow offered this warning drawn from an experience confronting her boss in a direct manner:

Being very direct with someone, and they took that as an affront, and took it negatively. Which I was shocked about, because I had always been able to be very forthright and honest in my counsel...I was reprimanded for being so forthright. So, I didn't do it that way anymore.

Several other female executives, including this PRSA Fellow, were wary of, and often avoided, using emotional appeals. As one female PRSA Fellow said:

I try to avoid emotional appeals. Primarily because of sensitivity to being a woman in a leadership position and the stigma about women being emotional in the workplace, and I probably erred in the other direction, but I never wanted to appear emotional about a discussion or base it on feelings.

Another mistake a male public relations executive said he made was issuing an ultimatum when he happened to walk in on an office affair:

And I said, "You know, you're risking the reputation of all of us with this behavior, and if you don't tell our boss, I'm going to tell our boss." I drew that line in the sand and I regret it. ...I started with an ultimatum instead of ended with an ultimatum. (Neill and Drumwright 2012)

Timing also can be a crucial factor when confronting a senior executive as this professional advised:

I think playing real close attention to their body language as you're speaking with them. If you sort of get the feeling that they want you to leave the room, I would buy some time. I would say, could we meet later in the day about this? I'd really like to talk to you about it. Maybe get a meeting later in the day. And then go back and spend some time thinking about and maybe even getting outside counsel about this issue, how we might approach it. He's not seeing the danger in the same way that I'm seeing it, so how can I get his attention? (Neill and Drumwright 2012)

A PRSA Fellow agreed that any confrontation is all about timing and the proper setting. She offered these words of caution:

> You learn there are ways to push back. You might not want to con-front a senior executive when he's surrounded by a bunch of his peers. But just circle back after the meeting or go see him before the meeting to say, "I'm going to raise this. Will you help me or will you chime in or I want you to be aware of it." So you don't put yourself in a confrontation where the guy's got to save face by firing you.

Likewise, she added it is not a good idea to confront a senior executive in a group e-mail, describing how a junior employee was almost fired for doing so.

> I had a gal who pushed back on a top executive of the company that bought us. And he wanted to get her fired immediately. "Who is this person?" And I had to go say, no, no that's one of my best people. And he was like…how dare her.

The Choice to Remain Silent

Results from the PRSA Fellows and SPRF survey revealed that almost 24 percent of the public relations executives had chosen to remain silent when faced with an ethical dilemma. When asked why they chose not to speak up, five reported fear of losing a job, five selected not enough evidence, two indicated it would not have made a difference, and two attributed their decision to not being a member of the decision-making team. The interviews provided additional insights regarding the decision to remain silent. One PRSA Fellow blamed it on inexperience and youth, "I was stunned and frozen, not having a clue what to do and what to say and feeling very young in the profession." Another PRSA Fellow regrets the early-career decision even now:

> I was young and I thought I could trust my leaders. And so when they said, "We're doing great. You know we're not going to go through bankruptcy. We're going to be fine." And so I believed

them. Looking back on it afterwards I thought they just lied. They just lied. And the writing was on the wall and I was so Polly-Ann-ish, so naïve, which is one reason they may have kept me and let others go. But I just—I trusted them so much that it was probably a failure in my maturity, my professional maturity at the time. I won't ever make that mistake again. One thing I did learn is that when your executives stop listening to your counsel, it's time to go.

Summary

Some senior public relations executives have mastered the art of raising ethical concerns to senior leaders in a nonconfrontational manner. One of the most common approaches involves simply asking probing questions and listening to understand the reasoning behind the decision, which also helps these executives develop counterarguments. Other approaches include using research, case studies, and legitimacy appeals, often tied to the organization's core values. Specific tactics include using the "headline test," providing alternatives, and raising the issue from the perspective of key stakeholders. The senior executives also warned that often, certain tactics such as issuing an ultimatum, confronting a boss in front of others, or attacking someone in a group e-mail could cause irreparable damage.

Questions to Ponder

1. Which of the influence strategies or tactics would you feel most comfortable using and why?
2. Why do you think men and women sometimes tended to use different influence strategies?
3. Why do you think the use of influence tactics varied by years of experience?

CHAPTER 5

More Powerful Together...
Recruiting Allies and
Forming Coalitions

One of the biggest challenges young professionals face may very well be properly navigating the internal politics within their organization. Part of the difficulty is business executives do not like to talk about and/or often deny it exists. Organizational politics refer to activities that are carried out with the purpose of acquiring and using power and "other resources to obtain one's preferred outcomes in a situation in which there is uncertainty or dissensus about choices" (Pfeffer 1981, p. 7). Allies and coalitions are examples of relational sources of power (Berger and Reber 2006). Coalitions can be either a hard or soft influence tactic, depending on whether it is employed in a straightforward and open environment, or characterized by "clandestine work behind the scenes to quietly gather the support of others" (Berger and Reber 2006, p. 116). A PRSA Fellow preferred to use both approaches:

> First I got permission from my boss, and then I created this group that I told you about. I called it crisis prevention committee. And they would tell me things in confidence and my office had walls, so that was nice, where they could come in and tell me what's really going on, so that we could be proactive and prevent crises.

This chapter focuses on the second type of coalition building (i.e., soft influence tactic), which involves informal conversations with colleagues throughout the organization to build support for certain positions or count the votes before a meeting. Fortunately, the public relations executives interviewed have provided a glimpse into how to use internal politics in ethics counseling by recruiting allies or forming coalitions.

The process begins with building relationships with colleagues throughout the organization, and choosing allies among "those with whom they interact frequently and with whom they feel comfortable" (Eisenhardt and Bourgeois 1988, p. 758). A VP of corporate communications for a Fortune 500 company believed this was fundamental to effective public relations:

> Informally, I had to work very aggressively, horizontally across the enterprise to get people to buy into my ideas, to support my ideas, and in many cases I ultimately learned that I needed to let go of my ideas and let somebody else take them, which felt very odd, very, very odd. So kind of informally, that's how things get done… even now we joke about we don't care how we get the ball in the end zone as long as we score. (Neill 2014, p. 602)

This same senior executive provided a specific example to illustrate the point. Two business units, he recalled, were making decisions inconsistent with company values and external communication. Corporate Communications and Marketing worked together on market research that ultimately supported their arguments:

> We realized that our business leaders were listening to us, but we didn't have the ball all the way punched into the end zone, and that we were going to have to exert more influence to get this stopped. And so formally, we went to the research team. Informally, we went to other influencers inside the company…like the chief communications officer, like the head of risk [management], like the general counsel, and just asked them to start asking questions. And the rest of it took care of itself, but we needed people in positions of higher authority than us…we also realized that our influence sometimes has limitations, and so we had to find— we had to educate others and get them as fired up about it as we were…because it was a peer-to-peer discussion. (Neill 2014, p. 602)

As this example illustrates, people create coalitions when "they do not have the power to change the organization independently or want to avoid the political consequences associated with unilateral action" (Murnighan and Brass 1991, p. 289). Senior executives with veto power must be included in successful coalitions, and they are often likely to be among the first invited to participate (Murnighan and Brass 1991). Neill (2014) found informal coalitions were used even in companies where public relations had a direct reporting relationship to the CEO. These informal coalitions were connected to public relations' internal boundary-spanning role, its need to monitor activities throughout the organization to be pro-active and therefore effective. Neill (2014) found public relations executives serving in leadership roles at the division level in the company identified issues at their level, but they lacked the authority to address them. For that very reason, they reached out to people serving in more senior positions as allies or formed coalitions with influential leaders from a variety of departments as a means to enhance their influence.

Based on accounts like the one described above, public relations executives need to develop political astuteness in identifying who the key decision makers are in each situation, their strengths and weaknesses, personal preferences, and their motivations (Berger 2005; Spicer 1997). One PRSA Fellow maintained it was a matter of developing an appreciation for their colleagues' challenges:

> Understand the concerns from their point of view, whatever their professional practice area...their fears about the outcome, whether it is personally or professionally. Will I look bad, will I look stupid? Will I look like a crook if I do this and such? What is the potential long-term fallout versus the pain today? A lot of us want to avoid the pain today and it causes bigger problems down the road...I go back to really listening to everybody's interests and what their concerns and fears are and how it might affect their ability to do their work or do their job or be successful. And how can we be ethical and frequently how can we be transparent about something without it hurting them and can I help them get there.

Identifying Allies

Being politically savvy also means knowing who sits on influential committees and how decisions are made in an organization (Berger and

Reber 2006; Pfeffer 1992). Complicating this effort is the reality that venues for discussing an ongoing issue may shift from boardrooms to hallways, individual offices, and coffee shops making it difficult for public relations executives to stay informed (Berger and Reber 2006). This reality requires public relations executives to "anticipate arena shifts and insert themselves into the process, or try to create information briefing sessions with key decision makers" (Berger 2005; Berger and Reber 2006, p. 730). A VP of corporate communications for a Fortune 500 company described how his department found a way to insert themselves into the decision-making process:

> Every either new solution or major change that we might be making to a product or service is centrally managed by this product management committee. So there are 100 product managers... there are 12 people on this committee. We don't sit on the committee, but we've actually gone from being at the tail end of the pipe...to all the way upstream where...we have two places in their process where they have to get through brand [and reputation committee] and PR before someone who's coming up with a new product or service can proceed to even get funding. (Neill 2012, p. 42)

Being politically savvy also involves identifying influencers within the company or organization and choosing the best ways to approach them. The case study involving the Fortune 500 company mentioned at the start of this chapter also offered insights regarding the communication channels that were used. As the VP of corporate communications recalled:

> Over lunch, catching people at the Starbucks. We have two Starbucks inside here. I got some work done down in the fitness center; we have four fitness centers, and in drive-bys or texting...and saying I need to catch you on something can you call me on your drive home, because I know I can't get to him [senior executive] during the day; he's booked from 6:30 a.m. to 7 p.m., but I know when he goes home. So text me on your way home or call me on your way home. (Neill 2014, p. 603)

While this example may seem unusual, in reality allies and coalitions are a routine influence technique used by public relations professionals. In response to surveys with members of the PRSA College of Fellows and SPRF, 55.6 percent said they had recruited allies or formed coalitions, and the most common partners were executives working in legal, human resources, and operations. A member of the Page Society made relationships a priority from day one:

> Anyone in communications immediately upon arriving in your job, it's all coalition building...I came out of a political background, so I knew that if you wanted to get something done you had to have a grassroots strategy. I would go into every organization saying who's in senior management. I may be too junior to know who the chief legal officer is, but I guarantee you that she has direct reports that I can find ways of working with. So I would seek out opportunities to network. I would make sure that if for instance there was something to be written...find out a way to go meet with that person. My philosophy being if they know you, they can't distrust you. You immediately build a relationship bridge when you meet the person.

As a new professional, building relationships with colleagues in other departments might seem a little intimidating. A PRSA Fellow urged young professionals to overcome their anxiety:

> You should make friends with corporate counsel or their equivalent outside. If you are a junior person I know that might be difficult, but if you are working for [a] senior communications manager perhaps you could suggest for your own benefit and growth if it is possible to sit down and meet with them and learn more about their department, do a little job shadowing informally. Lawyers are great mentors. That is the first place I would go.

Allies also are important for staying informed and limiting surprises, which is why one PRSA Fellow said this is so critical to public relations' environmental scanning and issues management roles:

They're essential. You can't do the job and certainly can't be an advisor without having those allies who are going to give an early heads up or warning of issues that might be coming. The sooner you can be involved in the discussion, the more likely you are to influence it, so you don't have a critical juncture where you're making decisions and digging in your heels.

One public relations executive working in education said he has relied on allies as a form of influence throughout his career:

This particular individual had a deep seeded distrust of communications people for whatever reason and so be it. But I also figured out very quickly that another person on our staff, another senior member, did have his ear and did have his confidence. And so what I learned to do was when I wanted to get an issue floated and get approval for it, was use this other person to go through. I just sort of knew instinctively that I would never be able to have that kind of trust and cooperation, but I could still get my job done letting somebody else take the ball, get the credit for it. I don't care who gets the credit for it as long as we can get the things done. (Neill and Drumwright 2012)

He added that allies can improve your personal credibility as well:

Every one of my bosses always has been willing to second guess me. Whenever I say something, they turn to their trusted counsel, whether it be legal counsel or whoever it may be, and say, "What do you think about it?" And the cool thing is when that individual says, "Yes, I agree"…and all of the sudden, they're going, the PR guy actually is saying things that match what the other people who I know and trust, so it's a matter of building your own credibility within the organization. (Neill and Drumwright 2012)

Recruiting Allies

There are different approaches public relations executives can use for recruiting allies. A PRSA Fellow once shared a book chapter with a colleague in human resources to begin the discussion:

So I asked her to read it...so that we could then discuss it, because I felt as if—for us to help move a significant change initiative in that organization, we were going to need to be forthright...So by giving her this chapter to read, and by setting up the time to then discuss it, and to talk about who else should we get involved... she helped because she was not only my boss, but she also was a member of the key leadership team. So she enabled me to present this point of view as well as to conduct some research among the leadership team...We did not have legal sitting at the table with us at that point in time, but what happened is if you have a complete leadership team that's bought into the direction as we did, then we became an influencer of legal, and then...we were stronger in terms of our arm wrestling with legal versus if it was just me or her or somebody else.

Senior executives provided several recommendations for new professionals who might be intimidated by the idea of recruiting allies, including this approach from a member of the Page Society:

I would say allies are critical. I mean especially the first couple of times you do it. You don't want to be the lone wolf. And so I would suggest starting with your boss and hopefully your boss is ethical and just saying, "Hey, there's something that doesn't sit right with me. Let me tell you what I'm seeing and perhaps you can help me make some sense of it"...In a non-threatening way...I frequently like that "hmm, this just doesn't seem right to me" approach rather than accusatory is probably early on in your career or probably throughout your career the better approach.

Recruiting allies does not typically happen through electronic communication. As a PRSA Fellow said, "Well, it's not the kind of thing you do by e-mail. You sit down face-to-face and eyeball to eyeball, and there are times when it might be a telephone conversation if someone's not in the office." Allies are especially critical when you are new to an organization and have not built the necessary relationships. As a member of the Page Society advised, "If you have to bring in a negative early on then

I would usually get an ally who knew them better and do it. I wouldn't just coldly go into somebody I'd never met before." This advice is consistent with Conger's (1998) recommendation to reach out to colleagues with high credibility to champion a position when you have yet to develop the necessary reputation and relationships.

In the situation described below, forming a coalition allowed executives to share information and piece together what was really going on. Consistent with the concept of social capital, Nahapiet and Ghoshal (1998) pointed out that new knowledge can be created by "combining elements previously unconnected or by developing novel ways of combining elements previously associated" (p. 248). *Trust* is essential for these information exchanges to occur (Nahapiet and Ghoshal 1998), as this PRSA Fellow explained:

> I was gathering data, and as I began to ask for copies of emails, substantiating evidence from people who might have been involved in certain things, they kind of began to wonder what do you need this for? And with a number of them, it became clear that they saw what was going on too. And they said, "Well, let me show you what I've got." And so actually there were a couple of us that went to the business ethics resource together, because we were each getting a different picture, but when we put it together, it became very clear what was going on.

This situation escalated into some of the employees serving as whistleblowers. Last resort influence tactics such as rocking the boat and whistleblowing will be discussed more in Chapter 6.

Summary

Public relations executives need to be politically savvy when it comes to understanding how decisions are made in an organization and who the key influencers are for a given issue. They routinely engage in private conversations with colleagues in other departments to determine where their colleagues stand on an issue prior to meetings and to build support for a decision that is consistent with the organization's values and mission.

As a natural progression, they often recruit allies and form coalitions with others who share their views as a means for enhancing their influence. Allies also help public relations professionals piece together important information and resolve issues before they become a crisis.

Questions to Ponder

1. Based on the accounts in this chapter, how would you go about recruiting allies?
2. What are some circumstances that public relations executives might face that may require them to recruit allies as a means of influence?
3. How would you identify who to approach as a potential ally? What characteristics would you find beneficial?

CHAPTER 6

Last Resort Approaches... Rocking the Boat and Whistleblowing

Sometimes ethics counsel falls on deaf ears. When that happens, public relations executives have three primary choices: (1) drop the issue and recognize the reality that they are not the final decision maker, (2) raise the concern to someone else, or (3) remove themselves from the situation by looking for another job or resigning. Senior public relations executives reported choosing all three of these options depending on the situation.

One PRSA Fellow described her obligation this way:

> When I have spoken then I'm not listened to—at least in all clear conscience I can say that I brought it forward...that's just part of the business and sometimes there are other powers at play that are going to make those decisions, but at least in clear conscience I can say, here's what I think, and here's why I think that and here's how I think that we should move forward.

Jones (1991) provided insight on why people may decide to raise ethical concerns in some circumstances and choose not to in others. He identified six components of moral intensity that may provide insight into what may motivate some people to resort to drastic measures and why others choose to remain silent. The first is *magnitude of the consequences*, a perspective that focuses on the potential harms or benefits of the act in question. He suggested that issues have to reach a certain threshold to inspire people to act. The second component is *social consensus*, which refers to the degree of social agreement that a proposed act is evil or good. Specifically, this means that in situations where actions are clearly unethical or illegal by societal standards, people may be more willing to speak up and oppose the action. The third component is *probability of effect*, which refers to both the likelihood that the act in question will take place and that harm or benefit will occur. The fourth component is *time*. When there is less time pressure, the moral urgency to act immediately is reduced. The fifth component is *proximity*, or how near we feel to the victims or beneficiaries (i.e., stakeholders) of the act in question. Jones (1991) emphasized that "people care more about other people who are close to them than they do for people who are distant" (p. 376). The final component is *concentration of effect*, or the number of people affected by the decision. Consistent with moral intensity, a public relations executive working in a nonprofit said:

> You have to pick your battles carefully. Over some minor thing, you don't want to fall on your sword. But the major ethical things, you just literally have to take a stand and draw a line in the sand. Like I say, you have to be prepared to walk out. (Neill and Drumwright 2012)

When the issue is highly illegal or unethical, and moral intensity is greater, some public relations executives resort to the Omega tactics we listed earlier, such as leaking information to the media or government regulators, sabotaging implementation of a decision, or serving as a whistleblower (Berger and Reber 2006). Using a scale of 1 to 5 with one being very unlikely and 5 being very likely, members of SPRF and the PRSA College of Fellows were asked how likely they were to use these various Alpha and Omega tactics (see Table 6.1). Based on their survey responses, the average score was 1.46 for leaking information externally, 2.41 for serving as a whistleblower, and 2.59 for using an internal anonymous reporting system.

Through other survey research focused on dissent tactics, Kang and Berger (2010) found similar results, reporting that the tactic of assertively confronting management about the inappropriateness of the decision was used in organizations where top management did not appear to be committed to ethics, and the tactic of agitating others to join them in arguing and working against the decision (i.e., allies and coalitions) was used in

Table 6.1 Preferred influence tactics

Type of influence tactic	Likelihood to use
Asking questions/listening/dialogue	4.67
Use of scenarios/alternatives/solutions	4.47
Research	4.27
Legitimacy appeals	4.23
Raise concerns of stakeholders	4.10
Headline test	4.09
Personal experiences	4.06
Case studies	4.00
Allies/coalitions	3.59
Direct approach	3.57
Pressure/persistence	3.53
Emotional appeals	3.20
Internal anonymous reporting system	2.59
Whistleblower	2.41
Leaking information externally	1.46

organizations lacking a code of ethics. They determined that sabotage and information leaks were rarely used.

Dissent is defined as "a multi-step process that involves: (a) feeling apart from one's organization (i.e., the experience of dissent), and (b) expressing disagreement or contradictory opinion's about one's organization (i.e., the expressions of dissent)" (Kassing 1997, p. 312). Articulated dissent refers to when employees raise concerns to someone within the organization who has the authority to address the concern such as supervisors and senior executives (Berger and Reber 2006; Kassing 1997). Someone who assumes the role of a dissenter does so "on the basis of (personal) principle and conscience" (Shahinpoor and Matt 2007, p. 40). Shahinpoor and Matt (2007) stressed that dissenters demonstrate their loyalty to the organization by voicing their concerns and advocating for improvements while still employed. When describing different forms of dissent, Redding (1985) defined a boat-rocker as someone "who expresses dissent—in a direct straight-forward manner—*within* the organization" (p. 246). By contrast, a whistleblower "voices his or her protest to people *outside* the organization" (Redding 1985, p. 246). During the interviews with PRSA Fellows, six reported serving as a whistleblower while ten said they had helped, advised or protected a whistleblower. In addition, three members of the Page Society said they had served as a whistleblower, and three of the Page members had helped, advised or protected one. Some of these executives started by raising the issue within the organization, or rocking the boat, and later had to resort to whistleblowing when those attempts failed to produce ethical action.

A member of the Page Society said she has been willing to raise the issue to someone higher in the organization, but always notified her colleagues before moving to the next level:

> Ok, I've brought this to your attention, I still feel really strongly about this. Know that I'm now going to escalate it to the next level, right. Because I don't want anyone to be surprised, because in one case I did go to the CEO and when the CEO called the person, I didn't want the person to not say, oh yeah, I never heard from [her name] on this issue.

Some companies and organizations have ethics hotlines or committees that allow employees to report ethical concerns. Public relations executives caution, however, that those systems are not always safe to use. In one situation, described by a PRSA Fellow, the ethics committee ultimately reported to the CEO, who happened to be the one engaged in unethical behavior. It was costing the company millions of dollars:

> I noticed that there were some conflicts of interest happening within the C-Suite and I reported it to the business ethics program and I reported it to the legal department, and nothing happened, except that I was reassigned to somebody else and basically sidelined. And as a senior practitioner, they brought in somebody who was 20 years my junior and basically started to assign my work to her. And they didn't fire me, but they completely put me in a closet. And I watched as my duties eroded and was so frustrated because I thought this is so wrong. And people throughout the company realized what was going on and felt this is so wrong, but nothing was happening.

She stressed the retaliation led to a chilling effect that discouraged others from speaking out:

> For these behaviors to be happening so blatantly and at the top levels, it was really shocking to a lot of people, and the fact that is was going unchecked and it was allowed to just happen. So there was a lot of public perception of wrong doing at that point. But no one felt empowered to be able to do anything about it without fear of losing their jobs. And especially when they saw the retaliation that I got that complicated things.

Eventually, she sought counsel from a mentor, who just happened to be friends with some of the members of the board of directors:

> He knew that I was very upset with my current work situation. And he said, "What is going on?" And I told him. I said, "In the deepest confidence, here's what's going on"...I said, "This is one of the few times in my career, I don't know what to do. I don't know how to influence this."...And finally after a number of discussions, he said, "Well, if I ever have the opportunity I know the chairman really well. You know we go play golf from time to time, and if the opportunity arises, I might just drop a bug in his ear." It was about five months later that I got the call that said the CEO's stepping down. And what makes me think that this guy had a hand in it was the very next day, I got a voice mail from him and he said, "Well, hope you're doing Ok. Hope this makes your job better." And he never said I did it, but it was like he was telling me it's been taken care of.

PRSA Fellow Paula Pedene and one of her colleagues agreed to let their names be used to describe their experiences as a whistleblower. Since the issue involved the health and lives of U.S. veterans, she and others were willing to speak up. She discussed the progression:

> We saw managers continuing to do things that were hurting our veterans. After those internal channels and anonymous letters didn't work I collaborated with Dr. Sam Foote to expose the wrong

doing through external sources, and that included Congress and the media. These avenues were very effective. It was a sad day for VA. But it was a good day for our veterans, because that's when the VA wait time scandal broke.

Another PRSA Fellow expressed gratitude for her moral courage:

This woman performed one of the great services to the veterans of America of which I am one and, you know, she got the attention finally after three years of being personally pilloried. Long story short, I defend people who do that, I just hope they're working in organizations where they don't have to do that.

PRSA named Pedene as their 2015 "Public Relations Professional of the Year."

Obviously, the decision to become a whistleblower requires courage and can come with great personal cost such as demotion and loss of employment. One PRSA Fellow felt a painful isolation:

Your network kind of shrinks, because at those points and times… two to three things happen. (1) You learn quickly who your true friends are. (2) You learn that there are people out there that are willing to throw you under the bus in order to help themselves get ahead. So there are people that don't worry about a cost to another human in order to advance their own selves, which I have always thought was just interesting. And (3) there's another group that out of fear cannot come forward to assist you.

Another PRSA Fellow had her motivations questioned when, as a volunteer board member, she presented evidence that senior leaders of a nonprofit organization had embezzled money to the point the organization was almost insolvent:

Many people on the board thought that I was kind of like a whistleblower and that I was trying to do it for some kind of personal gain. So it was an awkward situation to be in. To discover what you discovered, to tell people what you discovered. To have the facts there. Have the financial statement. The auditing firm. To have everything there to prove that you're right and that people felt that I was grandstanding.

And yet another PRSA Fellow said he "rocked the boat" when other members of a nominating committee seemed determined to fix an election:

The chair of the nominating committee went around and said, "Just so we're clear, does everyone agree with the path forward?" And it came to me, I was like one of the last people, and I said, "Absolutely not." I said, "I will not agree to this. This does not reflect the values of the university and I'm appalled at the suggestion of it." And I went to the president's chief of staff, who was also at the time serving as the ethics officer. And yeah, it didn't go well for the rest of the committee, but I was not going to be a party to it...It prevented something that I thought was very unfair from happening. And by the way, that person that they wanted to put up as the candidate, did not get elected.

Another PRSA Fellow spoke out when he witnessed harassment in the workplace. "So there was a situation where there was…a senior person, a vice president at the company whose behavior toward subordinates was so disturbing that I felt like I couldn't keep quiet about it." He ended up leaving the organization:

The official channel to go to in terms of the chain of command was not the proper way to go in this because of personal relationships. But others on the executive team…I felt like they got the message about what was going on. It was one of those things where in the short term, I felt some pain, but in the long term, I felt pretty good about it.

A Page Society member also spoke up about harassment in the workplace involving her boss:

I had a direct supervisor who did not model the values of the company at all by any stretch of the imagination and was absolutely abusive to my employees and I believe created a hostile work environment. And I took it to HR, I took it to ethics, I took it to the president of the company. I used every avenue I had available to me. They all chose to do nothing about it, and I had employees that went on stress disability. I had employees quit. It really was an awful, awful situation. And I weighed back and forth whether or not I should – I mean many, many times I wanted to quit, but then I felt like I was abandoning my employees and I was the only buffer they had, and what would happen if I left.

In that same situation, she encouraged other employees to report their personal experiences of harassment using the ethics hotline. She now says she wishes she would have left the company sooner.

Another situation that inspired a Page member to speak up involved an office affair involving a senior executive:

I made the information known only because it was affecting the performance of the company. I deem that kind of extramarital stuff unethical, but many people don't. But it was affecting the performance of the company and morale and all kinds of things.

He said he would share the information with the media or other influencers rather than using official internal reporting channels.

Yet another PRSA Fellow chose a different path. "I didn't move forward on it, because I needed more information, but in order for me to get more information I would have exposed what I was trying to find." This PRSA Fellow did not disclose the specific type of ethical dilemma that she faced, but only that she chose not to pursue the issue.

A few of the PRSA Fellows interviewed also described times when they provided counsel to potential whistleblowers. One PRSA Fellow said she encouraged employees to use resources inside the organization:

One of the directors for a recreation facility in the parks department was unethical, and it was clearly illegal and ultimately was convicted at that time and in jail for it. But there was several people who had access to that information and had witnessed what was going on and actually kept a diary. They came to me because I was a PR person and I strongly suggested that they work within the management team of the parks department and talk to HR and talk to legal counsel and encouraged them to speak the truth and tell them what ultimately was going on and impacting the facility in a negative way.

Another PRSA Fellow, while serving on a nonprofit organization's board, actually encouraged an employee to report an issue:

I was on the board, and we heard directly from an employee of things that were happening in the organization. And I honestly considered really calling the ethics line and saying I think this needs to be investigated. And I actually asked the employee, have you called the ethics line and asked for this to be investigated? And the employee felt that if she did that there would be retaliation against her...I brought it to the chair of the board and then the investigation was conducted that way.

Sometimes the publicity that comes from experience as a whistle-blower has led others to reach out for counsel:

One of the things that I didn't know was going to happen was once I became known as a whistleblower the number of people that would contact me. Yeah, so I have provided advice and counsel to numerous people regarding steps they can take, people that I know are good—legal representatives, good employee representatives. I have given them advice on moral courage, because a lot of times these people are being punished for their exposures, and it's something you have to deal with, because in the government especially it takes a long time for these cases to come to court, sometimes two to three to five years. So that's a long time for a person to be out of their job, humiliated, being picked on for an ethical disclosure. So it takes a lot of—in my own personal case, a lot of prayer helped, a lot of talking to people I could trust.

Though rare, another Omega tactic as discussed in Chapter 4 was observed—public relations executives leaked information to or tipped the media. One PRSA Fellow said she told reporters to examine her organization's financial records:

> I recommended to members of the news media, suggested to members of the news media to look into financial records and public documents that I knew an organization was withholding and not for the right reasons. The organization had tried to alter or edit an audit to make themselves look better, and it wasn't the case. So I suggested that they might want to scrutinize certain other available material and match it up and they could connect the dots for themselves, and they did.

Others have chosen to resign when faced with highly unethical behavior in their companies or organizations. One PRSA Fellow said it became increasingly obvious that it was time for her to go. "I did end up retiring younger than I wanted to just because...I just couldn't live with it anymore. I stayed three years after these guys bought us, but I just couldn't take it anymore."

While fear of retaliation or loss of one's job is a real concern and potential barrier to ethics counsel, one Page Society member said that does not change our obligations:

> Too many people focus on keeping their job not doing it. In these situations, you can't be afraid. You can't be focused on keeping your job. You focus on doing it. And doing your job means being that voice of reason, having convictions, telling the truth.

Another Page Society member added, "There are worse things than being fired." In support of that claim, he described his experience working for a company that was under investigation by the U.S. Securities and Exchange Commission for accounting fraud. While he was not in a senior management role at the time, he said:

> I'm not proud of my service there during that era. I'm proud of eight of the other 11 years that I was there. But those were

particularly dark days. Even though I wasn't directly responsible, I bear some of that. And so the notion is that once you start making compromises, it leads you down a dark and very difficult path. Even if you extricate yourself from it later, it's something that it will either sit on your conscience or quite frankly could inhibit your career down the road. My counsel is speak your truth. Have the guts to do it. You have to be smart about it, and be sensitive and thoughtful and fact based in how you do it. And don't compromise in those areas, because they can come back to bite you.

Summary

Public relations professionals tend to resort to Omega tactics only when Alpha tactics fail to produce change and when the activity is highly unethical or illegal. Based on their personal accounts, some began their efforts inside the organization, raising concerns to more senior executives or reporting issues to a hotline or ethics committee. When those efforts were unsuccessful, some reached out to members of the board of directors, mentors, government regulatory agencies, or the media. However, those who became whistleblowers did so at a high personal cost. Some lost their jobs, were demoted, or were socially isolated by friends and colleagues. Others chose to resign rather than continue to fight daily ethics battles.

Questions to Ponder

1. Under what type of circumstances did public relations executives resort to "rocking the boat" or whistleblowing?
2. What types of internal resources did the public relations executives mention using to report ethical concerns? What are the limitations associated with those systems?
3. What is moral intensity and how does it influence public relations executives' likelihood to resort to more drastic measures?

CHAPTER 7

How to Prepare for Ethics Counsel: Mentors, Training and Other Resources

Senior public relations professionals have learned that the advice and guidance of a trusted mentor can be invaluable to effective ethics counseling. Formal mentoring relationships typically partner a more experienced executive with a junior employee, and informal mentoring relationships develop more organically through the consent of both the mentor and protégé (Jablin 2001; Tam, Dozier, Lauzen, and Real 1995). Most public relations professionals have several mentors, sometimes for different stages in their careers. When examining the impact of mentors in the academic environment, Peluchette and Jeanquart (2000) found that professors in their early and mid-career stages who had mentors from multiple sources (e.g., formal internal and informal external) experienced the highest levels of both objective (e.g., research productivity) and subjective (e.g., work role, interpersonal, financial, life) success. By contrast, professionals in later career stages benefited more from internal mentors. As might be expected, more senior professors were less likely to have mentors (Peluchette and Jeanquart 2000).

Young professionals can find mentors through professional associations such as PRSA or by personally reaching out to a respected member of their local communities. Many of the senior executives we spoke with agreed with this PRSA Fellow that a crucial characteristic desired in a mentor is experience:

> It's important to have ethical mentors who are more senior than you, because the more seniority somebody has in this case, the more experience they're going to have in dealing with ethical concerns. I don't think this is a place where you can have an ethics

mentor who's the same age as you or younger when you're trying
to learn.

Through survey research with Millennials who are associate members of PRSA and members of the "New Professionals" section, Neill
and Weaver (2017) found 69 percent of the participants have a mentor
with whom they could discuss ethical concerns, and almost 63 percent
indicated they would be comfortable discussing ethical concerns with
a mentor who did not work at the same organization. The study also
revealed that Millennial practitioners who have a mentor were signifi-
cantly more likely to report that they felt prepared to offer ethics counsel
compared to those who do not have a mentor. Finally, "Millennials who
have confidence (e.g., are comfortable discussing ethics concerns with
supervisors, mentors, and clients) are more likely to provide ethics counsel" (Neill and Weaver 2017, p. 342).

Another related resource for young professionals, as one PRSA Fellow
pointed out, is their own professional network.

I...have reached out to other colleagues, you know PRSA's great
for that. You build a network of other professionals and as we
know, there's a right way to handle things, but there's more than
one way to be right. And getting opinions from others I find is
quite valuable...How would you handle this? Or have you ever
faced this? And what can I expect on day two, day three, day four?

Another public relations professional said formal mentoring relationships are not always required:

I didn't have a mentor, but I had colleagues and I could bounce
ideas off of them...When I was a junior pro, I could learn from
the senior pros by watching and asking questions of them as well.
And reading the paper and...seeing the mistakes people made and
then watching the pros and going hey, they handled that well and
learning from observation. (Neill and Drumwright 2012)

Accreditation

One source of ethics training that was often described as a milestone in many of the senior professionals' careers was studying for the accreditation exam (APR). The Universal Accreditation Board (UAB) is a partnership between nine professional associations (http://praccreditation.org/), which administers the APR exam. Both PRSA and SPRF are members of the UAB. Ethics and law account for 13 percent of the questions on the computer-based exam, and many senior executives, including this PRSA Fellow, strongly recommend that young professionals make plans early in their careers to take it when ready:

> I think that studying for the APR exam with its requirements for you to understand the code in-depth and be able to speak to it are amazing and will stand a professional in very good stead going forward in their career.

A senior executive working in higher education said studying for the accreditation exam helped him understand how ethics fits into the bigger picture:

> I don't want to say because I'm accredited I'm an ethical strategic professional, but I think that the process of accreditation—going back to the idea of ethics oftentimes being paired with something else...whether there's evaluation or research, whatnot. But I think that accreditation was one of those things in my professional career that helped me connect the dots between those more readily. I mean I knew that research was out there, I knew the evaluation was out there, I knew ethics was out there, but I think accreditation...put it all together in more of a color pallet as opposed to just a spattering of different assets or tools or whatnot, in the public relations industry...I think it's important to understand that ethics doesn't have a singular place in that process, but should be integrated into each of those major steps of the public relations process. So I did feel like accreditation to a strong degree

has probably helped me articulate the need for ethics much better than I could have before. (Neill and Drumwright 2012)

Recent survey research provided evidence and support for the value of ethics training as the results showed that *accredited* professionals were more likely to say they personally felt prepared to provide ethics counsel and to report that they were likely to provide ethics counsel when compared to the general PRSA membership (Neill 2016a).

While not a formal requirement, most PRSA leaders would recommend that public relations professionals have a minimum of five years of experience prior to taking the APR exam. Rather than waiting five years, however, recent graduates can still prepare by taking the *Certificate in Principles of Public Relations* (CPPR) exam. Ethics and law account for 12 percent of the questions on the CPPR exam.

Other Training

Some of the senior executives we spoke with, including the Page Society member below, reported that their employers provide ethics and compliance training or provide support for them to attend professional conferences:

> Being in financial services, I had to take a lot of internal ethics training and compliance training every year…I would attend ethics seminars again predominately with Ethisphere, which is how I got to know them. They have a global ethics summit every year that I would go to, and there would be others.

A survey of PRSA members revealed, unfortunately, that 63 percent of the respondents were not offered ethics training through their employer (Neill 2016a). Approximately a third, however, reported participating in ethics professional development programming provided by PRSA, with the most common examples including accreditation (24.6%), chapter meetings (24.3%), and webinars (14.8%).

In response to our latest survey, SPRF members equally rated college ethics courses, employer training, and religious upbringing as their

Table 7.1 Most common sources of ethics training

SPRF members	PRSA College of Fellows
College ethics course—17	APR exam—29
Employer training—17	Chapter meetings—23
Religious upbringing—17	PRSA conferences—23
Personal study—14	Personal study—20
APR exam—12	Employer training—15
Chapter meeting—11	Religious upbringing—15

most common sources of ethics training, followed by personal study, and the APR exam (see Table 7.1). Members of the PRSA College of Fellows listed the APR as their number one source of training, followed by PRSA chapter meetings, conferences, and personal study.

Other Resources

While it should come as no surprise that many senior professionals regularly consult the PRSA *Code of Ethics*, several of them also said they read the ethical standards advisories (ESAs) produced by the PRSA Board of Ethics and Professional Standards (BEPS). One PRSA Fellow recommended that professionals check the advisories routinely:

> I think the first step is going to the PRSA best research and see what the particular standards are and they continually upgrade and change those because of sociology and the society changes. For example, there's a new one out I believe in the last year or so on social media, and how you deal with social media in various areas. So the study of ethics by itself is not a static study, and I'm glad BEPS generally upgrades their advisories to find out where the issues are.

Other resources available on PRSA's website include case studies, an ethics quiz, and app. In addition, PRSA annually recognizes "Ethics Month" each September by sponsoring various webinars and Twitter chats and publishing blog posts about ethics.

Another resource that was mentioned by professionals, and the PRSA Fellow quoted below, is the Institute for Public Relations website (www.instituteforpr.org), which includes blog posts and research reports:

> I would certainly go to the Institute for Public Relations and see what kind of case studies they have on a particular kind of issue and see how the issues may jive or be separate and apart from the kind of things I might be confronted with, so absolutely on both the research and the case studies.

Another PRSA Fellow pointed to the Arthur W. Page Society (www.awpagesociety.com) as a helpful resource:

> I'll cite them again, because a lot of the content they put out is not just about how to—what is the chief communications officer of the future going to look like, but they're very much about the integrity of the profession. And there's a lot of people that blog in Arthur Page, and they write white papers, and they do things that really raise the bar very high. And I like that, because that just educates yourself about what other people think...how should people be handling these types of situations when they arise? Some of them are quite sticky and you don't really always know the right thing to do.

Personal Reflection

While all of these resources can be helpful, senior executives also recommend that young professionals take time for personal reflection and self-inventory, an exercise endorsed by this PRSA Fellow:

> I would have them [students] know what ethics is, I would have them know what their own code of ethics is, what PRSA's *Code of Ethics* is, so that those values are inside them...if the values are not their values, then they don't see it as an ethical issue. So they've got to line up their own values. And it's all reflective and internal.

Another Fellow recommended a rigorous personal assessment, as tough as it might be to complete:

> You start with yourself and you have to do a self-inventory, did I ever lie, did I ever cheat, did I ever steal? Pretty much everybody is going to have to say yes to those. But then it's looking—so what have you learned about yourself with regard to doing those things…and in effect you have to decide yourself first that you are going to be…straight and narrow with regard to ethics. And only then can you start to teach somebody else about ethics, the code and the right things. And I think you have to have a framework of values and whether it's PRSA values or your own, you need to sort of mush together, but the whole thing starts with the value statement in your head, and then I think that it's a degree of honesty that says well Ok, I made some mistakes in the past, but I'm going down the straight and narrow now.

Ethics training and personal assessments are not enough, though, according to a senior professional working in a nonprofit organization, who emphasized that they must be paired with a strong work ethic:

> I think it's an everyday thing. You're there; you're engaged in the organization or the company. Obviously, you're working for the good of the company or the organization, that's not questionable. There's no performance issues at all, you're meeting your goals and objectives or exceeding them, that all builds your cache, your credibility within the organization, which helps you to become eventually a trusted adviser. (Neill and Drumwright 2012)

Summary

Public relations professionals rely on a number of resources to help them provide ethics counsel. On a personal level, many consult mentors or their professional network to seek advice when faced with difficult decisions. Several senior professionals said personal study for the APR exam was as a turning point in their career in understanding ethics in public relations. Other ethics resources they use include the PRSA *Code of Ethics*, ethical standards advisories, and professional development opportunities such as conferences and webinars. Finally, public relations professionals should regularly complete a self-assessment to make sure they are acting ethically and that their job performance is meeting or exceeding expectations.

Questions to Ponder

1. How would you go about identifying and recruiting a mentor?
2. What is the value of accreditation for ethics training?
3. What types of free ethics resources are available online?

CHAPTER 8

Being Proactive: How to Build an Ethical Culture

Providing ethical leadership in public relations involves more than just speaking up when an issue arises. Senior public relations executives and professionals engage in more proactive initiatives as well. Companies and organizations now routinely promote their core values as a means of distinguishing themselves from others, a trend referred to as employer branding (Ambler and Barrow 1996; Foster, Punjaisri, and Cheng 2010; Lloyd 2002; Moroko and Uncles 2008; Neill 2016b; Vallaster and de Chernatony 2005). Business leaders have increasingly understood there is not only a need for establishing a brand, but also an even greater need to protect the brand. Employer branding efforts are motivated by desired outcomes such as employee recruitment, retention, engagement, and loyalty.

These outcomes require employee professional development and training opportunities, promotion or advancement potential, competitive salaries and benefits, and a sense of belonging and purpose (Ambler and Barrow 1996; Backhaus and Tikoo 2004; Berthon, Ewing, and Hah 2005). Employer branding communication campaigns are focused on communicating to current and prospective employees that it is a great place to work (Lloyd 2002). Neill (2016b) defined employer branding as the "promotion of core values to build employee identification and an ethical workplace beginning with employee recruitment and orientation followed by routine communication and rewards systems" (p. 7). Core values are "deeply ingrained principles that guide all of a company's actions" and serve as "cultural cornerstones" (Lencioni 2002, p. 6). Some examples of common core values include "collaboration, respect, honesty, integrity, humility, character, innovation, workplace safety, and customer service" (Neill 2016b, p. 11). One Page Society member said that core values should be well understood and adopted by employees throughout an organization:

> In this day and age with the intensity of transparency and social media, and immediacy and the 24-hour news cycle and the boundless, borderless geography, you simply do not have time to have a conversation for the first time [about] who are we and what do we believe in and what are our values. Those have got to be established and everybody has to understand and everybody has to be empowered with what those values are and what is the sense and purpose of this company and then it becomes very, very clear, and you don't have those debates.

In a previous study, Sison (2010) found that the CEO, often in collaboration with the executive team, develops the core values as part of a strategic planning initiative and then makes revisions, occasionally with the support of communication professionals. The two stages when communication executives have the most influence are (1) when they develop communication strategies and programs to promote those values, and (2) then distribute those messages through events and newsletters. These two stages are often completed in collaboration with human resources (Sison 2010).

Neill (2016b) examined the trend of employer branding through in-depth interviews with 32 communication executives specializing in internal communication. These communication responsibilities also were discussed with the PRSA Fellows and Arthur W. Page Society members who participated in the current study. One Page Society member said this is a core responsibility:

> As CCO's [Chief Communication Officers], our role is basically to be a conscience counselor that ensures the company's actions match its rhetoric, that our values are practiced and not merely preached, and really that the company's behaving responsibly and transparently with the interests of all the stakeholders in mind.

Based on the personal accounts of internal communicators, Neill (2016b) identified six best practices that companies and organizations should adopt to promote an ethical culture (see Figure 8.1):

1. Employers should communicate ethics in a culturally relevant way through employee testimonials and historical anecdotes.
2. Employers should review their core values to identify any inconsistencies with their policies and reward systems and then make necessary revisions.

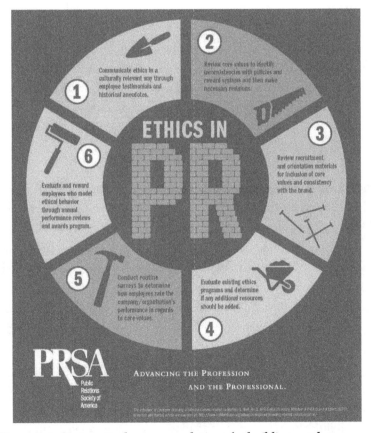

Figure 8.1 Six practical recommendations for building employer branding

Source: Graphic created by Arlington/Roe and Co for PRSA's Board of Ethics and Professional Standards. Used with permission.

3. Employers should review their recruitment and orientation materials for inclusion of core values and consistency with their employer brand.

4. Employers should evaluate their existing ethics programs and determine if any additional resources should be added.

5. Employers should conduct routine surveys to determine how employees rate the company/organization's performance in regards to their core values.

6. Employers should evaluate and reward employees who model ethical behavior through annual performance reviews and awards programs (p. 3)

These six ideas, as practiced by the professionals interviewed, provided a set of tactics to promote an ethical culture. Some of these tactics are employed by public relations executives and their staff. Others, however, require collaboration with colleagues in other departments.

Routine Communication and Anecdotes

Scholars have stressed that employers must communicate their values and ethics because "if people do not hear about ethics and values from the top, it is not clear to employees that ethics and values are important" (Trevino, Hartman, and Brown 2000, p. 135). Ethical leadership is defined as "the demonstration of normatively appropriate conduct through personal actions and interpersonal relations, and the promotion of such conduct to followers through two-way communication, reinforcement and decision-making" (Brown, Trevino, and Harrison 2005, p. 120).

Some of the most common communication tactics that reinforce core values include employee newsletters, town hall meetings, lunch and learn sessions, and posters (Neill 2016b). One Page Society member said his responsibilities include training and routine communication about ethics and values:

A lot of the counsel I provided was in helping create the ethics training and reinforcing the corporate values, making sure that we had the corporate values front and center in the internal comms, making sure that we identified people who were living our corporate values and highlighted them in our internal magazines and on the intranet and even social media once that became a thing, and so a lot of that counsel was just really finding those stories so that we could help other employees become aware with how we expected everybody to behave.

This description highlights two key responsibilities of public relations executives: (1) routine communication about ethics and core values and (2) using storytelling as an effective tactic. Neill (2016b) found internal communication executives created editorial calendars to help them consistently reinforce core values, while also routinely verifying that all communications that should include core values do so. Storytelling, whether conveying a positive or negative narrative, can be an effective tool in those efforts. One VP of communications relied on positive content to emphasize values, "We are always building feature narrative or feature editorial coverage…and then also using case studies of employees and of managers who are really demonstrating our values or bringing our values to life" (Neill 2016b, p. 14). By contrast, a Page Society member said his department provided examples of unethical behavior, such as employees not paying for cafeteria food, as reinforcement:

We have a number of self-serve kiosks for food, and we talk about there have been recourse when people will fake paying for food, when they're not really paying for the food, so they're stealing it. We can't have that. So we talk about real-life situations that are hard to comprehend that they actually happened. And so it's kind of hard to tell a story like what I just described. You mean to tell me somebody inside this building fakes paying for food? But that has happened. And so we talk about it. So we take the uncomfortable scenarios and talk about them very plainly and very directly with all employees. And every single all employee meeting and every meeting…leads with our mission and our standard.

Another Page Society member maintained that communication executives, using their strong language skills, can give meaning to abstract concepts like values:

This is where the communications person can really help is making it, defining it, helping an organization define it. But if they do it by themselves, they don't have the backing of the leader, the senior leader, then it will go nowhere. So it has to be something that has meaning within the organization. They get it, they know why it's there, and that could solve a lot of problems and help people understand how it applies to their daily lives.

Public relations professionals also can use their creativity to bring attention to ethics. One Page Society member described how they developed a screen saver using a map theme:

We saw it as a journey and the ethical piece is a journey and how do you find your way…So we created a screen saver with a little map that kind of danced around the screen to promote this and then we surprised the entire organization with the screen saver. So we didn't tell anybody it was coming. They happened to walk back from a meeting, what's that going on on my computer? What is that? So they had to look at it. They had to think about it. And it lasted a minute. That's much more effective than sending out a memo.

Reviewing Core Values for Inconsistencies

Stevens (2008) pointed out that "the mere existence of a corporate code of ethics does not prevent acts of egregious behavior" (p. 603). To be effective, core values need to be clearly communicated and embedded into the culture (Stevens 2008), meaning the code of ethics is actually used to make decisions, that those who behave consistent with the code are rewarded, and that leaders actually model behaviors consistent with the code. This PRSA Fellow said she has learned that is not always the case:

Too many organizations go through these vision and values exercises, and they create a list of values that in some cases they are merely platitudes and they make a nice poster on the wall, but nobody is living them and…I always assume it is my job rightly or wrongly to challenge those values and also to make sure that… are they being lived as well as we possibly can align and live them.

When companies and organizations promote core values, but do not follow them, it can lead to employee disengagement. As mentioned in Chapter 3, a chief marketing officer said her organization faced that risk when it emphasized collaboration as a core value, but instead chose to reward individual achievements rather than teamwork.

Recruitment and Orientation Materials

Prospective and new employees are typically introduced to the company's core values during recruitment and employee orientation. While human resources has traditionally managed both of these efforts, Neill (2016b) found that corporate communications and marketing are now helping to develop some of the promotional materials, such as videos and brochures, used in those recruitment and orientation activities. One communications director explained that her organization's orientation programs have changed from a focus on compliance to culture:

> It was very poor…it initially was really just almost a compliance sort of orientation where you went through HIPAA [Health Insurance Portability and Accountability Act], you went through what your benefits were; you went through safety and security…So what we've done is looked at it from a content perspective, what is it that we want each employee to really focus on…we also want to make sure that they get sort of a history and because [name of employer] brand is so strong, an idea of just the magnitude of the importance of work that [name of employer]) has done over the years, so we have a pretty strong video…we've helped them make it more engaging. (Neill 2016b, p. 13)

Identify Additional Resources

Identifying and promoting core values are not enough. Employers also must recognize and remove barriers to ethical behavior. McDonald and

Nijhof (1999) recommended that employers evaluate five factors that can impact ethical decision-making. The first factor involves identifying existing norms and values and determining whether those are encouraging or discouraging ethical behavior (McDonald and Nijhof 1999). The other factors include examining the work environment, specifically the decision-making processes, the availability of essential resources, and employees' abilities to make ethical decisions.

Scholars recommend that employers offer a range of ethics resources for their employees including ethics training, a code of conduct, reward systems, ethics hotlines, an ombudsperson, routine ethics audits, and decision-making trees (Bowen 2004; McDonald and Nijhof 1999). One Page Society member listed several resources her company provided including a chief ethics officer who reported directly to the CEO, an ethics council comprised of several senior executives, annual ethics training for employees, an ethics coordinator or champion in each business unit, an anonymous hotline, and toolkits for managers. She said her company gave more than lip service to ethics:

> Be sure that you take action on ethical concerns. So we were very clear that we had a zero tolerance policy for ethical issues, and if you were found to be acting in an unethical manner that was grounds for immediate dismissal. That's pretty powerful too…You have to do the training and it's a great annual reminder, but if you don't see the behaviors modeled around you on a daily basis, and if you don't see your leaders taking action based on core values or ethical issues and talking about that actively—if you don't have that behavior in your organization, then all the training in the world isn't going to do you any good.

While some of these resources were in place, Neill (2016b) found others were not being provided by the companies and organizations that she studied, specifically ethics audits and decision-making trees. In Chapter 6, it was reported that some senior executives warned that internal reporting systems were not always safe to use. This Page Society member said his company now offers such protection:

We've got a new speak up policy. It talks about the responsibility and obligation that...employees have to report or point out things that they hear are wrong, and it is backed by a commitment from the organization that there will be no retaliation and you have nothing to fear if you point out something that's wrong. So it guarantees protection, and it's very firm. The expectation and obligation is to speak up and the guarantee is when you do so, you have nothing to fear.

Another Page Society member provided this recommendation regarding an internal reporting system:

It's really important to have an ethics department that reports to the board and not up through the leadership of the company, so they can truly be independent and that they have an investigative arm with an anonymous tip line. I have worked in companies where there was absolutely retaliation for people raising concerns. I saw it firsthand and it was the way it was structured. And so people couldn't raise concerns without other people knowing who raised those issues, and people will be moved out of positions or direct reports stripped away from them or there would be other retaliatory steps taken.

In companies and organizations without some of these ethics resources, senior public relations executives might want to collaborate with human resources and the senior executive team to enhance their programs. Some employers also may have ethics officers who provide oversight of ethics programs and resources, and in those cases, they should be consulted and involved in any improvement efforts.

Routine Surveys

In two different studies, communication executives reported that their organizations evaluate management's performance related to their core values through survey research with employees (Neill 2016b; Neill and Jiang 2017). As a human resources manager said:

I'll look at our values scores too. So our values are supposed to be integrity, courage, curiosity—I'll look to…say, "Alright, how are we doing here?" Because if we're struggling in an area it makes me wonder are we not communicating well? Are we not being honest? Or are we not being perceived as being honest. (Neill 2016b, p. 12)

A director of communications for a nonprofit organization agreed that survey research with employees helped the organization identify areas for improvement:

They did a staff survey just this past August, and one of the primary concerns that resulted from that staff survey was lack of internal communications. When you dig a little deeper into survey results, it's a lot more than just communicating and getting news out. I think it touches much more with issues of lack of training or lack of connecting with the core values, or getting folks involved and engaged. But I think that when the survey results came out, the senior management team realized "Wow, everyone's really concerned about lack of communication." (Neill and Jiang 2017, p. 854)

Neill and Jiang (2017) found that most of the communication executives they interviewed assessed the company's performance through the prism of its core values through several methods, the most common of which were biannual or annual surveys. Other feedback tools included focus groups, "pulse" surveys,[1] and employee resource groups. A Page Society member provided a clear description of pulse surveys as "small, short ones, 6, 7 questions maybe, and you're doing a group of people not the entire employee base, but enough to get a good sample to see how things are going." The pulse surveys were especially influential in encouraging management to be more forthcoming with employees about

---

[1] Pulse surveys are quick surveys involving a small number of employees to get a sense of the "pulse" or sentiment regarding the state of the workplace.

possible facility closures that might impact their jobs. As a member of the Page Society recalled:

> From the results of the survey, we could see that the employees were really having anxiety...we used that survey and the results as communicators to present to management, so that they would have a clear idea of the environment, and that helped them make the decision to go ahead and inform.

Another senior executive, a vice president of communication, said his organization relied on employee resource groups for insights:

> Employee resource groups are...pretty common in large companies. They are groups that are dedicated to specific topics or areas of interests for employees. So for example, we have a professional women's group, we have a group that addresses LGBT, we have a group for military individuals. So these are...diversity and inclusion type groups. But they're very very good. First of all, they're very active in my company, and secondly, they're a very good place for us to gather input and research ideas about engagement and communications. (Neill and Jiang 2017)

Evaluate and Reward Employees

Some employers reinforce ethics and core values through annual awards programs and performance evaluations. Human resources typically manages both of these programs, though public relations practitioners may produce content about the awards programs for newsletters, the intranet, or internal social media channels. A human resources manager described her company's specific efforts:

> Our recognition program is based on the values. So when someone receives an award or gets a nomination for an award, it has to be related to one of the values. And then we have values painted

all over the office on the wall, so those are the two big reinforcements. And then they're also…rated on the values in your annual performance review. (Neill 2016b, p. 14)

Similarly, the director of corporate communication for a global transportation company said core values are a part of every employee's annual performance evaluation:

It's almost not even an option. So when you get your job review, you're…bucketed in ways by your manager on how are you delivering passionately personal service? How are you with bringing in new ideas and getting on board with the new ways of doing things? How well are you executing your operations, in addition to your core expectations of getting goals and objectives completed?…It's more about the how you're going about doing what you're doing, versus just what you're doing…If you're getting them done, but you're burning everyone down to the ground to get them done, that's not the way we want to operate as an organization. (Neill and Jiang 2017, p. 858)

On the opposite end of the spectrum, employers also have to be willing to take action against unethical behavior. As a member of the Page Society recalled:

Our CEO, he had to let somebody go who was a beloved and well-respected leader, and he said, "This wasn't a hard decision. It was one of the easiest decisions I've had to make." If you violate our core values, you can't stay…there's disappointment, but there wasn't any anx [anxiety] or agony over the decision.

All of these efforts can gather beneath the umbrella of employer branding with a focus on developing both intellectual and emotional buy-in among employees so they are committed to the organization, live out the brand's values, and become brand ambassadors (Mahnert and Torres 2007; Thomson, de Chernatony, Arganbright, and Khan 1999).

Summary

Public relations executives' role in ethical leadership involves proactive efforts to promote and reinforce the organization's core values. This role involves collaboration with the senior leadership team and colleagues such as human resources and ethics officers. Six best practices describe public relations' efforts to cultivate an ethical workplace, all focused on creating an ethical culture and improving employee engagement and loyalty.

Questions to Ponder

1. What types of activities do public relations executives engage in to help promote ethics and values in their companies and organizations?
2. Which responsibilities associated with promoting ethics and values involve public relations executives' collaboration with others in their company or organization?
3. Which of the six recommendations would you feel prepared to advise your employer to adopt and why?

CHAPTER 9

Practical Advice from Senior Pros

Embedded in all the personal stories told by the senior executives and professionals interviewed are nuggets of wisdom shared throughout this book. There are some lessons that are so fundamental, however, that a full chapter is dedicated to them. The core themes include the importance of developing business literacy, mistakes to avoid early in your career, researching employers prior to accepting a job, and serving as a leader no matter your current level of influence.

Business Literacy is Essential

Much of the advice from these senior executives and professionals focused on this prevailing thought: that young professionals need to build business literacy generally, especially understanding of their industry specifically. For one Page Society member this challenge was personally clear when he found himself successfully arguing that his company spends millions to address a product safety issue, overcoming internal opposition:

> We had the lawyers saying we're not required to do it. The engineer saying, "Yeah, we can fix it. I can't guarantee it won't happen again." And there was an asking for a recommendation and I ultimately, forcefully argued for a buy-back that we needed to get the vehicles off the road...but basically, this was headed toward a situation that the brand would not live through if something awful happened. And to the company's credit, they ultimately went along with it, and we purchased all those vehicles at a cost of $150 million and destroyed them.

From that experience, this same executive realized an important lesson to guide any public relations career:

> I think they have to be framed in a business context that to solely address [the issue] from a social or ethical perspective without also framing the business issues makes it more difficult to win over a room full of business people. That would be my biggest recommendation, and also this is more of an ongoing challenge for senior communications people: really pick and choose your battles...There are plenty of communications executives that cry wolf every time there's an issue...usually there's only a small number of issues that truly tarnish the brand or create real ethical problems for a company.

Another Page Society member encountered a similar challenge when he convinced his CEO to pull a retail partner's product from store shelves after the partner launched a controversial advertising campaign. Again, millions of dollars would be lost, so he had to build a business case focused on limiting future losses:

> He [CEO] said "Walk with me." We walked down to the chief marketing officer's office, actually we ran into him in the hallway. And he said, "[Page Society member's name] has concerns about this. What do you think? How much do we have invested?" I think at that time we had already spent about $15 million, and we probably had a $50 million spend planned on it, so it was a lot of money. And he [CMO] said, "This is how much we have in." He [CEO] said, "[Page member's name] are you telling us that this is the right decision?" And I said, "Yep." He in one second after that pulled the product. "Get it out of the store." And we totally walked away from a substantial piece of business and lost a lot of money on the deal, but it was morally the right thing to do. In an organization that is steeped in doing the right thing, sometimes you just have to make sure that you build your case for why it's the right thing and management will buy into it.

In this situation, the Page Society member had readied a one-page summary for the CEO and backed his recommendation with angry letters from consumers. In addition, he described future consequences that the retailer could face, such as organized protests in its stores and a decline in sales. As these examples illustrate, public relations executives and professionals need to understand how to read financials and the financial impact of their recommendations. In a similar vein, a PRSA Fellow also recommended strengthened math skills:

> I also think a lot of public relations people get into our profession because hey, we don't love math. They don't like business. They do not want to crunch numbers. We are the "people people," right. If you are working especially in a corporate or business setting, you have got to understand those business drivers. It is important for you to find somebody who can give you a basic education or at least somebody you can go and ask questions of, because a lot of ethical decisions are made for monetary reasons and not for the right ones.

Some public relations professionals, like this Page Society member, are motivated to improve their business literacy by pursuing an MBA:

> One of the best things I did—well, two pieces of advice, one that is buried in the other. One is get as smart as you can about business, and how businesses are run, so that you can understand how decisions are made and the tradeoffs that a CEO might have to make in making some of these ethical decisions. And the second is for me, I went back and got an MBA to take care of number one. Within my MBA, I took an ethics course that was fascinating and it gives you a way of thinking about some of these things that is enlightening and in some ways makes you more perplexed, because one ethical issues aren't black and white. There are tradeoffs and it is who gets the greater good?

Others may prefer personal study, and one helpful resource to start that process is *Business Essentials for Strategic Communicators* by Matt

Ragas and Ron Culp (2014). There are also a number of helpful resources in the current Business Express Press collection ranging from business law, corporate governance, financial accounting, and human resources, just to name a few. Students and young professionals also should regularly read business and industry trade publications such as the *Wall Street Journal*, *Fortune*, *Bloomberg*, and *Inc.* to keep up with industry trends and terminology.

While the controversial ad campaign mentioned earlier in this chapter ended successfully for that Page Society member, he also remembered a time when as a young professional, he used the wrong approach. "I would lose most of the emotional arguments…and so early on I would go by a knee-jerk and thinking it was so rational and obvious that I can't understand why you're not agreeing with me." He now relies more on legitimacy and rational arguments grounded in data, and he advises young professionals to do the same:

> You don't want to be predictable that you're always going to say no. You want to be that person they come to for a discussion about here's what we're thinking. Pick holes in it if you can. So I always try not to be—I try to avoid that early stage where I was knee-jerking everything and no one was listening to me to being hey, this is someone who's going to give a thoughtful discussion. Before we walk out of the room, we're going to have a good discussion about what's possible and what we shouldn't do, so that's positioning.

One of the best ways to improve your expertise within an organization is by building *internal relationships*. This senior executive working in higher education said it is a simple matter of starting where you are:

> If I were to say looking at someone who's coming up in the field… start small. Maybe you can't get the visibility of the top people right off the bat. But find someone within your department within your operational area or someone slightly higher than you, and start building a level of trust. Then the word will start moving upward and people will start—the phone calls if you will—will

start. They will start calling and hey, we're having a meeting on such and such a topic and we'd like for you to be a part of the discussion…Not everybody is going to report immediately to the top guy, so start at the level of comfort, start at the level of accessibility and just stick with it. (Neill and Drumwright 2012)

A Page Society member recommended a bold approach:

I would go into meetings where I wasn't necessarily invited, and I'd say, "I'm really curious about how you're organized in the legal department, and could you kind of give me the ideas, so that if and when I ever needed to tap anyone I don't blindly just call you and if you happen to be out of town or a meeting"…Oh, my god, the chief legal officer loves that. First of all, they're shocked and confused at first because no one's ever done it. But then, "better idea, come to my staff meeting and then in turn, you tell me how you're organized in your function." And it opened all kind of doors—the trusting relationships…And you became this is an unusual PR person that actually cared about what we do.

These efforts then led to informal meetings around coffee and more influence:

I would call and say, "Hey, after the staff meeting do you want to have coffee?" And next thing I know I'm moving up the food chain to the level of significance within the organization. And then they start bouncing ideas off you.

These trusting relationships later allowed him to serve as bridge between the CEO and other senior leaders:

I'll never forget one case. This was after I reached the management level, and the CEO…relied on my advice and counsel. And the business runners, and even though they may never have worked with PR, they're calling me for coffee and they're telling me what's on their minds and then when I'm meeting with the CEO during my weekly meeting, I was like, so and so is concerned about this. He said, "He never told me that." I said, "He's afraid to. He's afraid you're not going to like the idea." He said, "It's not a bad idea." And I said, "I don't think so either." And he said…"Why isn't he telling me that?" I said, "No one wants to speak truth to power"…so I got these guys talking to each other.

Another Page Society member reached out to senior executives to find out how he could help them:

> What I used to do is do audits every single year of senior executives around the world: people stationed in Asia, legal executives and our CIO [Chief Information Officer], and really try and understand exactly what they were trying to accomplish, what is their strategy, what are their hurt barriers or challenges that they face and what role could communications play in being a problem solver, a solutions partner with them.

He added that relationship building takes time and requires political savvy:

> And if you can add value at both a macro-level, and what I mean macro is the whole corporation, and also add value at a micro-level or vertical level, which would be HR, legal, finance or ops [operations], then that to me is how you gain a seat at the table to be able to actively influence events and have some leverage with your point of view, because they trust you, they've seen you produce. They've seen the results. They know you're there to add value and they respect you, so you have to earn this over time both based on your conduct, being very empathetic to their business requirements and also I think being diplomatic in that you've got to know…how far to push and when to back off, but also using fact based arguments not just opinions, but facts, surveys, hard data, if you will, to back up your claim.

Another Page Society member cautioned that those who desire to be influential also must be willing to put in extra hours:

> It's amazing how many people want to just get up in the morning, come to work, show up at 8, go home at 5. The best conversations you're going to have are after 5 o'clock…if you're not there at 7 in the morning, 7:30, you're not going to have those private conversations with the CEO…if that's what you want, you can't have it. The work ethic issue is probably one of the biggest things that people have to realize will affect them and their abilities.

Mistakes to Avoid

While a strong work ethic will build your credibility, young professionals need to know that certain infractions can cause serious damage to their career. One Page Society member recalled an incident while attending a social event with fellow executives:

> One of the young people when the check came, we all divvied it up and paid separately. But then he reached over and grabbed the overall check and said, "If you don't mind, I'd like this, because this is as good as cash on your expense report." And so I was creeped out and I also was very young at the time. But fast forward a year, and I get promoted and then somebody comes to me and tells me that this is somebody they want me to interview for a job in my department.

He, of course, did not want to hire this person, because he did not trust him. The problem, this senior executive said, was that he did not report the issue when it initially happened, and later had to disclose to senior leadership why he was so reluctant to hire this person. "My lesson learned from that is I should have addressed it at the time rather than wait until it became a bigger issue." If he could do it over, this is what he wished he would have done:

I probably should have said (a) I just want you know how this looks, and I really think that you need to think twice before doing it, because (1) it's wrong, and (2) you just signaled to a large group of maybe impressionable people that this is acceptable, and it's not. And so in hindsight, I would have addressed the issue when it happened.

Another cautionary note regarding networking. While it is acceptable to build relationships over coffee, young professionals should be careful about alcohol consumption, as this professor with more than 40 years of experience in public relations constantly advises his students:

You go to a social thing, but you're there for business, you're there to either get an account or meet somebody or you're trying to get a job. I said, "I walk around with a glass of soda and a lime for the first hour and half. Everybody thinks it's vodka, but it's not." And I'm able to do my business. If I didn't do that, I wouldn't probably do it as well if I'd had a couple of drinks. So I say, "Schmooze, but don't booze." (Neill and Drumwright 2012)

One of the PRSA Fellows actually emphasized this lesson with a story about the time she and others lost respect for a colleague, after finding her passed out at a professional networking event: "And unfortunately, hurt feelings were involved. Relationships were destroyed…So, human behavior, on a personal level, instigated a lot of ultimately ill will, and an unfortunate set of circumstances and broken relationships."

Research Potential Clients and Employers

Senior executives and professionals caution that ethics counseling is challenging even when working with ethical employers and clients. That is why they advised young professionals to conduct extensive research prior to taking a job or signing with a new client. One professional working in the transportation industry shared a cautionary tale based on her experience with a previous employer. She resigned when asked by a vice president to put out false information in a news release. "They were saying all the right things on their website, and then their company literature, but there was no follow through." She added:

> Even though they had stated employee values in place, nobody adhered to them, and they didn't have a robust checks and balance...They had outsourced that to some 800 hotline that you could report, but there was little or no follow-up. (Neill and Drumwright 2012)

From each of these stories, it's easy to see why it is so important that young professionals not only conduct online research about potential employers, but also talk to employees who work there. High turnover rates can be a warning sign. This same public relations executive did not leave alone when she resigned over questionable activities. Others followed. She added: "Guess what, the lead attorney shared my views and assured me he wasn't going to let any funky stuff go on. But he was there all of three weeks." (Neill and Drumwright 2012)

A PRSA Fellow agreed that choosing an employer wisely makes all the difference:

> So much of it has to do with the moral standing and practices of the company that you work for...there are companies that I probably wouldn't want to work for. You're pretty much putting your job on the line every day. (Neill and Drumwright 2012)

A PRSA Fellow provided a cautionary note regarding clients in an agency setting, as she recalled a high-profile client that lied to her. Just being associated with that client for only two weeks caused her to lose clients and 10 percent of her revenue:

> Even though I've been in the business a long time, I'm accredited, I'm a Fellow...none of that, none of my academic credentials, none of my awards, my reputation, all of that was gone very, very quickly. Because I represented somebody who obviously, in retrospect, different lie, different story, every single day. The takeaway is that you have to be even more conscious of when people, when

you meet them, are they telling you the truth? What is their real objective in terms of having public relations representation?

The lesson—protect your own reputation and choose your clients and employers carefully.

Provide Leadership at Your Level of Influence

Young professionals who aspire to advance to more influential management roles should be encouraged by the advice provided by some Page Society members. As one of them counseled:

> One of the essences of leadership is it's not a function of position. It's not a function of titles. Again my counsel to young professionals is don't wait until you're promoted or promoted twice to feel like you can assume the mantel of leadership. Leadership is situational and corporations today need people to step into that role…they need to understand that generally the people who are willing to speak truth are the ones in my view that rise the fastest. And the other thing is…to operate with integrity and to know your craft and to know the facts. And if you can present your case in a strong fact-based way, people will listen to you.

Another Page Society member agreed with this perspective, "I think that we don't know how much permission we have to lead. And I think that we can lead at every level."

Excellent leadership in public relations "encompasses a complex mix of individual skills and personal attributes, values, and behaviors that consistently produces ethical and effective communication practice" (Meng, Berger, Gower, and Heyman 2012, p. 24). Through an online survey involving mid- and senior-level public relations professionals, Meng et al. (2012) determined that the top three qualities of excellent leadership are strategic decision-making, the ability to solve problems and produce desired outcomes, and communication knowledge and expertise. They added that to be an "excellent leader in public relations, one must know the organization's business and its environment, understand the decision-makers and decision-making process in the organization, and be proactive in that decision-making process" (p. 28). They found that young professionals can build their leadership skills through on-the-job experiences, personal initiative and desire, and observing successful role models.

Consistent with these findings, a Page Society member warned that public relations professionals at any level suffer if their advice is not accompanied by rigorous preparation. She described how she and another newly promoted colleague, a legal officer, felt unprepared when attending their first senior-level meetings:

> They were very much talking about operations-oriented things and other business issues that seemed real foreign to us. We didn't feel like we had total permission to contribute in that area and nothing could have been further from the truth. We came out of that meeting and then we went to another one. And we looked at each other and we said we have got to do something different. They did not bring us in, so that we sit there quietly and don't contribute. They don't need us, if we can't contribute.

Both she and the legal officer soon realized the need for pre-meeting preparation:

> We literally studied up on other aspects of the business and we knew what that agenda was well in advance, and we worked on different agenda points in terms of getting a better understanding of the things that they were talking about, so that we could have a point of view to contribute. And that's kind of hard, but a really important lesson...But finding your voice appropriately, not being a know-it-all certainly, but being informed and providing a point of view.

This same Page Society member described a time when she provided advice outside of her core responsibilities, advice that was eventually heeded. While there was no instant reward, her efforts were later praised by her boss:

In my performance review that year, my boss called that out and applauded me and said you had definitely nothing to gain. It was completely outside of your path. It was a fantastic recommendation, and because we were too inside our own boxes to see that there was lots of other options and we need to be addressing the needs of our entire management team and we weren't... You came up with a solution...That was a big lesson for me too. I didn't get a real pat on the back at the time, but then three months later in my performance review it was called out as showing leadership and being aware and thoughtful.

Leadership also involves *listening* to the concerns of various stakeholders. As this Page Society member explained:

You have to surround yourself with diversity of thought, because one of our most important roles is to be traveling in so many different circles and understanding so many different perspectives that we could actually give good counsel. What I find in the financial industry often is people are living in a bubble. And it's the PR counsel's role to remind the senior executives that their perspective is in a certain bubble, and it does not match the perspective of every stakeholder audience. So I think traveling different circles, like immersing yourself in different perspectives, voraciously reading...I always tell people—try to be as diverse in your thought and understanding as possible, understand different perspectives.

Listening to different global views regarding what is ethical is especially important when working for multinational companies and organizations. One Page Society member realized that when she and her colleagues in Europe initially found themselves on opposite sides of an issue:

It didn't take me very long to be educated by our European colleagues to recognize that just because it's legal doesn't mean we as a company don't have a moral obligation...because we're in the business of saving lives...I mean that for us was at the core of ultimately our point of view here. And I was looking at it from too U.S. centric perspective at the very beginning. Once I shed that view, and that requires hearing other points of view, whether it's your own internal colleagues or the broad employee base or external folks, but once you take in that perspective I think you can bring a much more grounded, values-based approach to your decision making and implementation.

In this situation, the company was able to reach a moral decision that was consistent with its core values and those of its global employees, and as a result they developed new industry practices related to product distribution that were adopted by others, a true example of ethical leadership and moral imagination.

Summary

Senior public relations executives provided some key lessons that young professionals should focus on early in their careers. First, new professionals need to build their business literacy. They can do so through advanced degrees, accreditation, personal study, and building relationships with executives in other departments. Second, they also need to avoid mistakes that can damage their career and credibility such as abusing expense reports and overindulging in alcohol at professional networking events. Third, young professionals also should research potential employers and clients before accepting a job. And, fourth, they can begin to provide leadership at their level of influence from day one. That leadership, however, demands research and viable solutions rather than knee-jerk reactions based on emotions and not grounded in facts.

Questions to Ponder

1. Which piece of advice did you consider most helpful and why?
2. What do you perceive are your gaps in business literacy and how can you begin to address those?
3. What resources can you use to build your understanding of a specific industry that you either work in or would like to work in the future?

CHAPTER 10

Conclusion: Everyday Practices

In 2015, the PRSA Board of Ethics and Professional Standards chose the theme of "Ethics Every Day" for their annual observation of ethics month. As the committee chair for ethics month that year, Kirk Hazlett, PRSA Fellow, explained in a blog post on PRSAY, "Ethics should be an everyday reality for all of us. It should be intuitive and proactive, not haphazard and reactive." We agree with that sentiment and would like to provide a list of ten recommendations that should be a part of every public relations executive and professional's routine. While work obligations may prevent us from completing these activities on a daily basis, these activities should be integrated on a weekly or at least monthly basis.

Being alert enough to recognize ethical concerns begins with taking care of your personal health at every level: physical, mental, and spiritual. Everyone needs plenty of sleep, a healthy diet, and regular exercise. For some executives and professionals, taking care of themselves will mean making time for prayer, reflection, or reading spiritual or motivational texts to help them stay connected with their personal values. After these personal needs are met, the following ten activities should be a part of your routine to help you make ethics part of your everyday life:

1. **Review your company, industry and/or PRSA code of ethics routinely.**

   PRSA has its *Code of Ethics* available on business cards that can be a quick reference guide when issues arise. A PRSA Fellow shares this card with colleagues:

   > I might pull out my PR ethics card and talk to them about you know the code provisions…when you start looking at things like competition and disclosure of information and free flow

of information or why that's important...to understand conflicts of interest and so forth. I think those are all things that help someone think about the bigger picture than just whatever might be the tactical assignment on that given day.

2. **Create a file of case studies by researching news stories, articles, and books for examples of good and bad ethical behavior by companies and organizations.**
Unfortunately, there is never a shortage of headlines regarding ethical *mis*conduct as this PRSA Fellow found:

> I have quite an extensive library of textbooks and Harvard Business Review case studies. I bookmark them or I keep them obviously very organized in my office. And if there's something that is similar to an issue that I'm facing, I'll be the first one to use case studies or look into my reference books to see what the case is, and what they ultimately decided to do and what the outcome was. I'm always a big research person. I like to find out what others have done before I start going forward.

3. **Check the PRSA website for new and updated ethics resources.**
While most public relations professionals are aware of the PRSA *Code of Ethics*, many are unaware of the other resources available including case studies, an app, ethical standards advisories, an ethics quiz, and webinars. This PRSA Fellow recommends the app:

> I think the ethics app, which is on the iPhone is always a good resource if you can't be around a computer and you get a question you know if you are out in the field someplace, besides the quiz is fun to take when you are waiting on something.

4. **Be alert and ask questions to identify any ethical concerns in your company or organization.**
To serve as an ethics adviser, public relations professionals need to ask the tough questions and identify decisions that might be problematic. A member of the Page Society added this important caveat:

There's times when you may not be given accurate information, and so then we thought our role was to always ask and ask as a reporter might ask, again give that different view, look around the corner, and try to keep the company on the right course.

5. Routinely participate in or attend professional development programs such as conferences, chapter meetings, and webinars that focus on ethics.

Everyone is busy, but new issues and trends emerge, and, as this PRSA Fellow advised, it is important for public relations professionals to pay attention to best practices:

> To prepare, young professionals need to attend and not ignore the ethics panels and programs that are put together by their local PRSA chapter. They need to become engaged in PRSA, so that they can learn the examples from others of how they have helped counsel people...I have found over the years that no matter what the topic is I almost always learn something from an ethics panel.

6. Read blog posts about ethics.

Some great resources include PRSAY and the Arthur W. Page Center for Integrity in Public Communication. Jim Lukaszewski, PRSA Fellow and member of the PRSA Board of Ethics and Professional Standards (BEPS), said that blogs are vital resources:

> Regularly reading blogs on ethics is essential to broadening your ethical competence for three reasons: Ethics discussions are always helpful because they inform you from your own perspective. Almost any ethics discussion will trigger fresh ideas you can use. You will always be ready with helpful, cogent, constructive, sensible, powerful, and influential comments on the spot just when someone (e.g., your boss) you are helping needs them.

Kirk Hazlett, a PRSA Fellow and former member of BEPS, said young professionals should not be shy. Do not just passively read blogs, join in the conversation:

> Knowledge is not a one-way street. Anyone who really wants to be well-informed on any topic should be aware of the conversations taking place relating to that particular area of interest. In today's communication universe, blogs are an excellent way both of knowing what is being discussed and of offering one's own thoughts and opinions to the conversation.

7. **Talk to respected mentors and senior colleagues about their experiences confronting ethical challenges.**
   As a PRSA Fellow said, "If you have an opportunity to talk to somebody you know who's been a leader…some of their life experiences can really help guide you, and listening to those life experiences can make a difference."

8. **Observe others' behavior, both good and bad, and learn from their successes and mistakes.**
   One Page Society member recommended that observation may involve learning from coworkers or newsmakers:

> It's important for young professionals to at least acquaint themselves with definitions and examples of good and bad ethical behavior. And I think the wiser they are about that the better counsel they can give. And I think reading as many case examples…case histories as they can, will help them see the consequences of poor ethical and good ethical behavior. They should certainly watch movies like "The Smartest Guys in the Room," the Enron case, or there's many documentaries now about ethical lapses.

9. **Make time to network and maintain relationships.**
   Almost every senior executive and professional we spoke with, including the following, said professionals must nurture relation-

ships with colleagues within their organizations who might be good allies or coalition members, while also setting aside time to network with industry colleagues who might also be good counselors:

> What's been beneficial to me, especially if I have a question about something, I've got a network of peers that are accredited, and that I respect, and they subscribe to the same beliefs and values as I do. And if I need a little help on something, and they can…talk you through it, 'cause, you're not out there by yourself. (Neill and Drumwright 2012)

10. **Look for opportunities to reinforce your organization's core values in routine communication.**
A Page Society member described his company's efforts in this area:

> We put original content on our intranet every day and every week we feature two to three employees that live our values and live the culture of doing the right thing the right way, and that's one aspect of it. There are a series of things that we do on an ongoing basis to remind people - to consistently tell the culture story…whether we feature our employees on our digital signage…in all of our major sites around the world. We have 50 major sites around the world.

He said they also provide front-line supervisors with toolkits to help them better communicate with employees, and while also spending roughly $25 million annually on training programs that address ethics and compliance issues and other related topics.

Even if your company does not have $25 million to dedicate to ethics training, there are other ways to reinforce ethics. This Page Society member said the efforts should be comprehensive:

> You need to have a variety of channels with employees to communicate your values and the company's values. And to do that with enough frequency in enough formats that people

just kind of believe it in their soul that it's part of the DNA of the organization. It's not about having a meeting and saying it or sending it in a memo. It's about living it and living it means truly living it day to day.

Summary

This is by no means an exhaustive list of recommendations, but it is a valuable starting point based on wisdom gained through experience and study. Some weeks we do better than others as deadlines and crises disrupt our best intentions. But, as these senior public relations executives and professionals counsel, we should always return to this routine. Even in our busiest of times, public relations executives and professionals have to take time to reflect and ensure that decisions are ethical and sound. Reputations, and therefore livelihoods, depend on it. We cannot allow pressures to compromise our integrity.

Questions to Ponder

1. Which of these 10 practices can you most easily adopt and why?
2. Which of these goals did you find to be most challenging to complete and why?
3. Can you identity other activities that should be part of a routine in order to practice ethical public relations?

APPENDIX A

Use of Influence Tactics by SPRF and PRSA College of Fellows

Type of influence tactic	SPRF		Fellows		Total	
	$n = 39$	%	$n = 33$	%	$n = 72$	%
Asking questions/listening/dialogue	28	72	30	91	58	81
Direct approach	26	67	26	79	52	72
Use of scenarios/alternatives/solutions	24	62	26	79	50	69
Legitimacy appeals	20	51	28	85	48	67
Raise concerns of stakeholders	22	56	26	79	48	67
Personal experiences	20	51	27	82	47	65
Headline test	17	44	24	73	41	57
Research	19	49	21	64	40	56
Case studies	13	33	21	64	34	47
Allies/coalitions	16	41	16	48	32	44
Pressure/persistence	10	26	18	55	28	39
Emotional appeals	12	31	11	33	23	32
Internal anonymous reporting system	4	10	5	15	9	13
Whistleblower	0	0	2	6	2	3
Leaking information externally	1	2	0	0	1	1

Use of Influence by Gender: College of Fellows and Page Society Combined

Type of influence tactic	Men		Women		Total	
	n = 29	%	n = 26	%	n = 55	%
Legitimacy appeals	25	86	21	81	46	84
Case studies	28	97	17	65	45	82
Allies/coalitions	23	79	21	81	44	80
Personal experiences	23	79	18	69	41	75
Pressure/persistence	16	55	21	81	37	67
Research	19	66	17	65	36	65
Emotional appeals (personal) or regarding stakeholders	10	34	11	42	21	38
Asking questions/listening/ dialogue	8	28	10	38	18	33
Use of scenarios/alternatives/ solutions	7	24	3	12	10	18
Direct approach	5	17	5	19	10	18
Whistleblower	2	7	7	27	9	16
Leaking information to media/ government officials/external influencer	0	0	3	12	3	5

APPENDIX C

Use of Influence by PRSA College of Fellows

Type of influence tactic	Men		Women		Total	
	n = 14	%	*n* = 20	%	*n* = 34	%
Case studies	14	100	12	60	26	76
Legitimacy appeals	10	71	15	75	25	73
Allies/coalitions	9	64	15	75	24	71
Research	10	71	14	70	24	71
Personal experiences	8	57	13	65	21	61
Pressure/persistence	5	36	15	75	20	59
Emotional appeals (personal) or regarding stakeholders	3	21	7	35	10	29
Asking questions/listening/ dialogue	4	29	7	35	11	32
Direct approach	4	29	5	25	9	26
Use of scenarios/alternatives/ solutions	4	29	3	15	7	21
Whistleblower	1	7	5	25	6	18
Leaking information to media/ government officials/external influencer	0	0	3	15	3	9

APPENDIX D

Use of Influence Tactics by Arthur W. Page Society

Type of influence tactic	Men		Women		Total	
	n = 15	%	*n* = 6	%	*n* = 21	%
Legitimacy appeals	15	100	6	100	21	100
Personal experiences	15	100	6	100	21	100
Case studies	14	93	5	83	19	90
Allies/coalitions	14	93	6	100	19	90
Pressure/persistence	11	73	6	100	17	81
Research	9	60	3	50	12	57
Emotional appeals (personal) or regarding stakeholders	7	47	4	67	11	52
Asking questions/listening/ dialogue	4	27	3	50	7	33
Use of scenarios/ alternatives/ solutions	3	20	0	0	3	14
Whistleblower	1	7	2	33	3	14
Direct approach	1	7	0	0	1	5
Leaking information to media/ government officials/external influencer	0	0	0	0	0	0

References

Abelson, R.P. 1982. "Three Modes of Attitude-Behavior Consistency." In *Consistency in Social Behavior: The Ontario Symposium*, eds. M.P. Zanna, E.T. Higgins, and C.P. Herman, 131–46. 2 Vols. Hillsdale, NJ: Lawrence Erlbaum Associates.

Aldoory, L., B.H. Reber, B.K. Berger, and E.L. Toth. 2008. "Provocations in Public Relations: A Study of Gendered Ideologies of Power-Influence in Practice." *Journalism and Mass Communication Quarterly* 85, no. 4, pp. 735–50.

Aldrich, H., and D. Herker. 1977. "Boundary Spanning Roles and Organization Structure." *Academy of Management Review* 2, 217–30. doi:10.5465/AMR.1977.4409044

Ambler, T., and S. Barrow. 1996. "The Employer Brand." *The Journal of Brand Management* 4, no. 3, pp. 185–206.

Backhaus, K., and S. Tikoo. 2004. "Conceptualizing and Researching Employer Branding." *Career Development International* 9, no. 5, pp. 501–17.

Berger, P.L., and T. Luckmann. 1967. *The Social Construction of Reality*. Garden City, NY: Doubleday.

Berger, B.K. 2005. "Power Over, Power with, and Power to Relations: Critical Reflections on Public Relations, the Dominant Coalition, and Activism." *Journal of Public Relations Research* 17, no. 1, 5–28. http://dx.doi.org/10.1207/s1532754xjprr1701_3

Berger, B.K., and B.H. Reber. 2006. *Gaining Influence in Public Relations: The Role of Resistance in Practice*. Mahwah, NJ: Lawrence Erlbaum Associates.

Berthon, P., M. Ewing, and L.L. Hah. 2005. "Captivating Company: Dimensions of Attractiveness in Employer Branding." *International Journal of Advertising* 24, no. 2, pp. 151–72.

Bivins, T.H. 1992. "A Systems Model for Ethical Decision Making in Public Relations." *Public Relations Review* 18, no. 4, pp. 365–83.

Bowen, S.A. 2004. "Organizational Factors Encouraging Ethical Decision Making: An Exploration into the Case of an Exemplar." *Journal of Business Ethics* 52, no. 4, pp. 311–24.

Bowen, S.A. 2008. "A State of Neglect: Public Relations as 'Corporate Conscience' or Ethics Counsel." *Journal of Public Relations Research* 20, no. 3, pp. 271–96.

Bowen, S.A. 2009. "What Communication Professionals Tell us Regarding Dominant Coalition Access and Gaining Membership." *Journal of Applied Communication Research* 37, no. 4, pp. 418–43.

Bowen, S.A. 2017. "How Can We End the Era of CEO Hubris." *PR Week*, April 21. Retrieved from http://prweek.com/article/1431208/end-era-ceo-hubris

Brown, M.E., L.K. Trevino, and D.A. Harrison. 2005. "Ethical Leadership: A Social Learning Perspective for Construct Development and Testing." *Organizational Behavior and Human Decision Processes* 97, no. 2, pp. 117–34.

Bunderson, J.S. 2003. "Team Member Functional Background and Involvement in Management Teams: Direct Effects and the Moderating Role of Power Centralization." *The Academy of Management Journal* 46, no. 4, pp. 458–71.

Burgoon, M. 1989. "Messages and Persuasive Effects." In *Message Effects in Communication Science,* ed. J.J. Bradac, 129–64. Newbury Park, CA: Sage.

Burt, R.S. 1992. *Structural Holes: The Social Structure of Competition.* Cambridge, MA: Harvard University Press.

Cialdini, R.B., and M.R. Trost. 1998. "Social Influence, Social Norms, Conformity, and Compliance." In *The Handbook of Social Psychology*, eds. S.T. Fiske, D.T. Gilbert, G. Lindzey, 151–92. 2 Vols. New York, NY: Oxford University Press.

Cohen, D.V. 1993. "Creating and Maintaining Ethical Work Climates: Anome in the Workplace and Implications for Managing Change." *Business Ethics Quarterly* 3, no. 4, pp. 343–58.

Conger, J.A. 1998. "The Necessary Art of Persuasion." *Harvard Business Review* 113, no. 3, pp. 84–95.

De George, R.T. 2009. *Business Ethics,* 7th ed. Boston, MA: Prentice Hall.

DiStaso, M., D.W. Stacks, and C.H. Botan. 2009. "State of Public Relations Education in the United States: 2006 Report on a National Survey of Executives and Academics." *Public Relations Review* 35, no. 3, pp. 254–69.

Dodd, M. 2012. *A Social Capital Model of Public Relations: Development and Validation of a Social Capital Measure* (Doctoral dissertation). Retrieved from http://scholarlyrepository.miami.edu/cgi/viewcontent.cgi?article=1829&context=oa_dissertations

Eisenhardt, K.M., and L.J. Bourgeois III. 1988. "Politics of Strategic Decision Making in High-Velocity Environments: Toward a Midrange Theory." *The Academy of Management Journal* 31, no. 4, 737–70. doi:10.2307/256337

Fitzpatrick, K.R. 1996. "The Role of Public Relations in the Institutionalization of Ethics." *Public Relations Review* 22, no. 3, pp. 249–58.

Fitzpatrick, K., and C. Gauthier. 2001. "Toward a Professional Responsibility Theory of Public Relations Ethics." *Journal of Mass Media Ethics* 16, nos. 2–3, pp. 193–212.

Fitzpatrick, K.R. 2002. "From Enforcement to Education: The Development of PRSA's Member Code of Ethics 2000." *Journal of Mass Media Ethics* 17, no. 2, pp. 111–35.

Foster, C., K. Punjaisri, and R. Cheng. 2010. "Exploring the Relationship Between Corporate, Internal and Employer Branding." *Journal of Product and Brand Management* 19, no. 6, pp. 401–09.

French, J.R.P., and B. Raven. 1959. "The Bases of Social Power." In *Studies in Social Power*, ed. D. Cartwright, 150–67. Ann Arbor, MI: Institute for Social Research.

Gioia, D.A. 1992. "Pinto Fires and Personal Ethics: A Script Analysis of Mixed Opportunities." *Journal of Business Ethics* 11, nos. 5/6, pp. 379–89.

Goodpaster, K.E., and J.B. Matthews. 1982. "Can a Corporation Have a Conscience?" *Harvard Business Review* 60, no. 1, pp. 132–41.

Goodstein, J.D. 2000. "Moral Compromise and Personal Integrity: Exploring the Ethical Issues of Deciding Together in Organizations." *Business Ethics Quarterly* 10, no. 4, pp. 805–19.

Grunig, L.A., J.E. Grunig, and D.M. Dozier. 2002. *Excellent Public Relations and Effective Organizations*. Mahwah, NJ: Lawrence Erlbaum Associates.

Grunig, J.E. 2006. "Furnishing the Edifice: Ongoing Research on Public Relations as a Strategic Management Function." *Journal of Public Relations Research* 18, no. 2, pp. 151–76.

Halff, G. 2010. "Codes of Conduct: Managing the Contradictions Between Local and Corporate Norms." *Journal of Communication Management* 14, no. 4, pp. 356–67.

Hazlett, K. 2015. "Ethical Practice Every Day: Who Cares and Why?" Retrieved from https://prsay.prsa.org/2015/09/01/ethical-practice-every-day-who-caresand-why/

Holtzhausen, D.R., and R. Voto. 2002. "Resistance from the Margins: The Postmodern Public Relations Practitioner as Organizational Activist." *Journal of Public Relations Research* 14, no. 1, pp. 57–84.

Jablin, F.M. 2001. "Organization Entry, Assimilation, and Disengagement/ Exit." In *The New Handbook of Organizational Communication: Advances in Theory, Research, and Methods*, eds. F.M. Jablin and L.L. Putnam, 732–818. Thousand Oaks, CA: Sage Publications.

Jacobs, J. 1991. "Moral Imagination, Objectivity, and Practical Wisdom." *International Philosophical Quarterly* 31, no. 1, pp. 23–37.

Jemison, D.B. 1984. "The Importance of Boundary Spanning Roles in Strategic Decision-Making." *Journal of Management Studies* 21, no. 2, pp. 131–52.

Jones, T.M. 1991. "Ethical Decision Making by Individuals in Organizations: An Issue-Contingent Model." *Academy of Management Review* 16, no. 2, pp. 366–95.

Kahn, R.L., D.M. Wolfe, R.P. Quinn, J.D. Snoek, and R.A. Rosenthal. 1964. *Organizational Stress: Studies in Role Conflict and Ambiguity*. New York, NY: John Wiley and Sons, Inc.

Kang, J., and B.K. Berger. 2010. "The Influence of Organizational Conditions on Public Relations Practitioners' Dissent." *Journal of Communication Management* 14, no. 4, pp. 368–87.

Kassing, J.W. 1997. "Articulating, Antagonizing, and Displacing: A Model of Employee Dissent." *Communication Studies* 48, no. 4, pp. 311–32.

Kelman, H.C. 1961. "Processes of Opinion Change." *The Public Opinion Quarterly* 25, no. 1, pp. 57–78.

Kennan, W.R., and V. Hazelton. 2006. "Internal Public Relations, Social Capital, and the Role of Effective Organizational Communication." In *Public Relations Theory II*, eds. C.H. Botan and V. Hazelton, 273–96. Mahwah, NJ: Lawrence Erlbaum Associates.

Kitchen, P.J., J.G. Spickett-Jones, and T. Grimes. 2007. "Inhibition of Brand Integration Amid Changing Agency Structures." *Journal of Marketing Communications* 13, no. 2, pp. 149–68.

Kochanska, G., and N. Aksan. 2006. "Children's Conscience and Self-Regulation." *Journal of Personality* 74, no. 6, pp. 1587–618.

Kohlberg, L. 1969. "Stage and Sequence: The Cognitive-Development Approach to Socialization." In *Handbook of Socialization Theory and Research*, ed. D.A. Goslin. Chicago, IL: Rand McNally and Company.

Lee, J., S.M. Jares, and R.L. Heath. 1999. "Decision-making Encroachment and Cooperative Relationships Between Public Relations and Legal Counselors in the Management of Organizational Crisis." *Journal of Public Relations Research* 11, no. 3, pp. 243–70.

Lee, S., and I. Cheng. 2011. "Characteristics and Dimensions of Ethical Leadership in Public Relations." *Journal of Public Relations Research* 23, no. 1, pp. 46–74.

Lencioni, P.M. July 2002. "Make Your Values Mean Something." *Harvard Business Review* 80, no. 7, pp. 5–9.

Lloyd, S. 2002. "Branding from the Inside Out." *BRW* 24, no. 10, pp. 64–66.

Mahnert, K.F., and A.M. Torres. 2007. "The Brand Inside: The Factors of Failure and Success in Internal Branding." *Irish Marketing Review* 19, nos. 1/2, pp. 54–63.

McDonald, G., and A. Nijhof. 1999. "Beyond Codes of Ethics: An Integrated Framework for Stimulating Morally Responsible Behaviour in Organizations." *Leadership and Organization Development Journal* 20, no. 3, pp. 133–47.

McGregor, D. 1960. *The Human Side of the Enterprise*. New York, NY: McGraw-Hill.

Men, R.L., and S.A. Bowen. 2017. *Excellence in Internal Communication Management*. New York, NY: Business Expert Press.

Meng, J., B.K. Berger, K.K. Gower, and W.C. Heyman. 2012. "A Test of Excellent Leadership in Public Relations: Key Qualities, Valuable Sources, and Distinctive Leadership Perceptions." *Journal of Public Relations Research* 24, no. 1, pp. 18–36.

Miles, R.H. 1976. "Role Requirements as Sources of Organizational Stress." *Journal of Applied Psychology* 61, no. 2, pp. 172–79.

Miltch, W.E., and D.M. Orange. 2004. "Conscience as the Reappearance of the Other in Self-Experience: On Using the Concepts Superego and Conscience in Self Psychology." *Psychoanalytic Inquiry* 24, no. 2, pp. 206–31.

Mitchell, R.K., B.R. Agle, and D.J. Wood. 1997. "Toward a Theory of Stakeholder Identification and Salience: Defining the Principle of Who and What Really Counts." *Academy of Management Review* 22, no. 4, pp. 853–86. doi:10.5465/AMR.1997.9711022105

Moberg, D.J., and M.A. Seabright. 2000. "The Development of Moral Imagination." *Business Ethics Quarterly* 10, no. 4, pp. 845–84.

Moroko, L., and M.D. Uncles. 2008. "Characteristics of Successful Employer Brands." *Journal of Brand Management* 16, no. 3, pp. 160–75.

Moss, D., G. Warnaby, and A.J. Newman. 2000. "Public Relations Practitioner Role Enactment at the Senior Management Level within U.K. Companies." *Journal of Public Relations Research* 12, no. 4, pp. 277–307.

Murnighan, J.K., and D.J. Brass. 1991. "Intraorganizational Coalitions." In *Research on Negotiation in Organization,* eds. M.H. Bazerman, R.J. Lewicki, and B.H. Sheppard, 283–306. 3 Vols. Greenwich, CT: JAI Press.

Nahapiet, J., and S. Ghoshal. 1998. "Social Capital, Intellectual Capital, and the Organizational Advantage." *Academy of Management Review* 23, no. 2, pp. 242–66.

Neill, M.S. 2012. *Seat at the Table(s): An Examination of Senior Public Relations Practitioners' Power and Influence Among Multiple Executive-Level Coalitions* (Doctoral dissertation). Retrieved from http://repositories. lib.utexas.edu/bitstream/handle/2152/22093/neill-dissertation-20126. pdf?sequence=1

Neill, M.S. 2014. "Building Buy-In: The Need for Internal Relationship Building and Informal Coalitions in Public Relations." *Public Relations Review* 40, no. 3, pp. 598–605.

Neill, M.S. 2015a. "Beyond the C-Suite: Corporate Communications' Power and Influence." *Journal of Communication Management* 19, no. 2, pp. 118–32.

Neill, M.S. 2015b. "Emerging Issues in Internal Communications: Generational Shifts, Internal Social Media and Engagement." *Public Relations Journal* 9, no. 4. Retrieved from http://prsa.org/Intelligence/PRJournal/Vol9/No4/

Neill, M.S. 2016a. "Accredited vs. Non-accredited: How Accreditation Impacts Perceptions and Readiness to Provide Ethics Counsel." *Public Relations Review* 42, no. 5, pp. 856–66.

Neill, M.S. 2016b. "The Influence of Employer Branding in Internal Communication." *Research Journal of the Institute for Public Relations* 3, no. 1. Retrieved from http://instituteforpr.org/influence-employer-branding-internal-communication/

Neill, M.S., and M.E. Drumwright. 2012. "PR Professionals as Organizational Conscience." *Journal of Mass Media Ethics*, 27, no. 4, pp. 220–34.

Neill, M.S., and E. Schauster. 2015. "Organizational Crossroads: The Intersection of PR and Advertising Ethics." In *Persuasion Ethics Today*, eds. M. Duffy and E. Thorson, 44–62. New York, NY: Routledge.

Neill, M.S., and H. Jiang. 2017. "Functional Silos, Integration and Encroachment in Internal Communication." *Public Relations Review* 43, no. 4, pp. 850–62. http://dx.doi.org/10.1016/j.pubrev.2017.06.009

Neill, M.S., and N. Weaver. 2017. "Silent and Unprepared: Most Millennial Practitioners Have Not Embraced Role as Ethical Conscience." *Public Relations Review* 43, no. 2, pp. 337–44. http://dx.doi.org/10.1016/j.pubrev.2017.01.002

O'Neil, J. 2003. "An Investigation of the Sources of Influence of Corporate Public Relations Practitioners." *Public Relations Review* 29, no. 2, p. 159.

Ots, M., and G. Nyilasy. 2015. "Integrated Marketing Communications (IMC): Why Does It Fail?" *Journal of Advertising Research* 55, no. 2, pp. 132–45.

Paluszek, J. 1989. "Public Relations and Ethical Leadership." *Vital Speeches of the Day* 55, no. 24, pp. 747–50.

Parsons, P. 2008. *Ethics in Public Relations*. London, England: Kogan Page.

Patterson, P., and L. Wilkins. 2005. *Media Ethics: Issues and Cases*. New York, NY: McGraw-Hill.

Peluchette, J.V., and S. Jeanquart. 2000. "Professionals' Use of Different Mentor Sources at Various Career Stages: Implications for Career Success." *Journal of Social Psychology* 140, no. 5, pp. 549–64.

Pfeffer, J. 1981. *Power in Organizations*. Marshfield, MA: Pitman.

Pfeffer, J. 1992. *Managing with Power: Politics and Influence in Organizations*. Boston, MA: Harvard Business School Press.

Piaget, J. 1997. *The Moral Judgment of the Child* (M. Gabain, Trans.). New York, NY: Free Press Paperbacks.

Ragas, M.W., and R. Culp. 2014. *Business Essentials for Strategic Communicators*. New York, NY: Palgrave Macmillan.

Raven, B.H. 1992. "A Power/Interaction Model of Interpersonal Influence: French and Raven Thirty Years Later." *Journal of Social Behavior and Personality* 7, no. 2, pp. 217–44.

Rawls, J. 1971. *A Theory of Justice*. Cambridge, MA: Harvard University Press.

Redding, W.C. 1985. "Rocking Boats, Blowing Whistles, and Teaching Speech Communication." *Communication Education* 34, no. 3, pp. 245–58.

Redmond, J., and R. Trager. 1998. *Balancing on the Wire: The Art of Managing Media Organizations*. Boulder, CO: Coursewise Publishing.

Rest, J., E. Turiel, and L. Kohlberg. 1969. "Level of Moral Development as a Determinant of Preference and Comprehension of Moral Judgments Made by Others." *Journal of Personality* 37, no. 2, pp. 225–52.

Rest, J.R. 1986. *Moral Development: Advances in Research and Theory.* New York, NY: Praeger Publishers.

Ryan, M., and D.L. Martinson. 1983. "The PR Officer as Corporate Conscience." *Public Relations Quarterly* 28, no. 2, pp. 20–23.

Schwartz, S. 1996. "Value Priorities and Behavior: Applying a Theory of Integrated Value Systems." In *The Psychology of Values: The Ontario Symposium,* eds. C. Seligman, J.M. Olson, and M.P. Zaana, 1–24. 8 Vols. Mahwah, NJ: Lawrence Erlbaum Associates.

Scott, W.R. 1981. *Organizations: Rational, Natural, and Open Systems.* Englewood Cliffs, NJ: Prentice Hall.

Shahinpoor, N., and B.F. Matt. 2007. "The Power of One: Dissent and Organizational Life." *Journal of Business Ethics* 74, no. 1, pp. 37–48.

Sison, M.D. 2010. "Recasting Public Relations Roles: Agents of Compliance, Control or Conscience." *Journal of Communication Management* 14, no. 4, pp. 319–36.

Spicer, C. 1997. *Organizational Public Relations: A Political Perspective.* Mahwah, NJ: Lawrence Erlbaum Associates, Inc.

St. John, B., III, and Y.E. Pearson. 2016. "Crisis Management and Ethics: Moving Beyond the Public-Relations-Person-as-Corporate Conscience Construct." *Journal of Mass Media Ethics* 31, no. 1, pp. 18–34.

Stevens, B. 2008. "Corporate Ethical Codes: Effective Instruments for Influencing Behavior." *Journal of Business Ethics* 78, no. 4, pp. 601–09.

Tam, S.Y., D.M. Dozier, M.M. Lauzen, and M.R. Real. 1995. "The Impact of Superior Subordinate Gender on the Career Advancement of Public Relations Practitioners." *Journal of Public Relations Research* 7, no. 4, pp. 259–72.

Thomson, K., L. de Chernatony, L. Arganbright, and S. Khan. 1999. "The Buy-in Benchmark: How Staff Understanding and Commitment Impact Brand and Business Performance." *Journal of Marketing Management* 15, no. 8, pp. 819–35.

Todd, V. 2009. "PRSSA Faculty and Professional Advisors' Perceptions of Public Relations Curriculum, Assessment of Students' Learning and Faculty Performance." *Journalism and Mass Communication Educator* 64, no. 1, pp. 71–90.

Trevino, L., L. Hartman, and M. Brown. 2000. "Moral Person and Moral Manager: How Executives Develop a Reputation for Ethical Leadership." *California Management Review* 42, no. 4, pp. 128–42.

Vallaster, C., and L. De Chernatony. 2005. "Internationalisation of Services Brands: The Role of Leadership During the Internal Brand Building Process." *Journal of Marketing Management* 21, nos. 1/2, pp. 181–203.

Wright, D.K. 1993. "Enforcement Dilemma: Voluntary Nature of Public Relations Codes." *Public Relations Review* 19, no. 1, pp. 13–20.

About the Authors

Marlene S. Neill, PhD, APR, is an assistant professor at Baylor University, and teaches courses in public relations and advertising.

Her research interests include public relations management and ethics. She has published 14 articles in journals such as *Journal of Media Ethics, Public Relations Review, Journal of Advertising Education, and Journal of Communication Management.*

Neill is an accredited member of the Central Texas Chapter of the Public Relations Society of America. She served as the chair for the Southwest District of PRSA in 2011. At the national level, Neill served a three-year term on the Universal Accreditation Board, which administers the examination for Accreditation in Public Relations; the Nominating Committee, which selects national board officers in 2012; and was appointed to the Board of Ethics & Professionals Standards in January of 2013.

She received her PhD in advertising from the University of Texas at Austin, her Master of Arts degree in journalism from the University of Missouri at Columbia, and her Bachelor of Science degree in journalism from the University of Kansas. Neill previously worked for almost 12 years in government and nonprofit public relations.

Amy Oliver Barnes, APR, After more than 20 years as a broadcast journalist, Amy Oliver Barnes moved to the public relations profession first as Public Relations Director at Arkansas Children's Hospital, then as Executive Director of Communications at the University of Arkansas at Little Rock. She received her master's in journalism from UALR in 1998 and joined the faculty in the UALR School of Mass Communication in 2006. Along with her extensive broadcast background, Barnes is an accredited public relations professional who has served on the executive board of the Arkansas Chapter of the Public Relations Society of America for more than seven years. She became chapter president in 2003, and later served as chair for the Southwest District of PRSA representing more than 2,000 members in six states, was a member of the PRSA National Nominating Committee, a national assembly delegate for six sessions, and chaired the PRSA National Research Task Force.

Index